HEALING WITH AROMATHERAPY

Healing with Aromatherapy

MARLENE ERICKSEN

KEATS PUBLISHING

LOS ANGELES

NTC/Contemporary Publishing Group

The purpose of this book is to educate. It is sold with the understanding that the publisher and author shall have neither liability nor responsibility for any injury caused or alleged to be caused directly or indirectly by the information contained in this book. While every effort has been made to ensure its accuracy, the book's contents should not be construed as medical advice. Each person's health needs are unique. To obtain recommendations appropriate to your particular situation, please consult a qualified health-care provider.

Library of Congress Cataloging-in-Publication Data

Ericksen, Marlene.
    Healing with aromatherapy / Marlene Ericksen.
       p. cm.
    Includes bibliographical references and index.
    ISBN 0-658-00382-8
      1. Aromatherapy. I. Title.

RM666.A68 .E75 2000
615'.321—dc21

                                       00-025005

Text Design by Laurie Young
Published by Keats Publishing
A division of NTC/Contemporary Publishing Group, Inc.
4255 West Touhy Avenue, Lincolnwood, Illinois 60712, U.S.A.

Printed and bound in the United States of America

International Standard Book Number: 0-658-00382-8

00 01 02 03 04 VP 18 17 16 15 14 13 12 11 10 9 8 7 6 5 4 3 2 1

615.321
Eric

To my mother, Anne, who taught me the wisdom of nature.

To my grandmother, Anna Borchek, and her grandfather,
who knew the healing ways of herbs.

And to my daughter, Ileana, who was being created
in the womb as this book was written, and who, I hope,
along with all children, will continue to have the privilege
of knowing the serenity and beauty of nature.

CONTENTS

Contents

x

PREFACE

You are about to embark on a journey into the wonderful world of aromatherapy. The use of aromas has a special place in the human saga. Scent has taken us to heightened planes of consciousness in temples of worship and through rituals of spiritual passage. Ancient Hindus anointed themselves with aromatic oils when worshipping to rid themselves of spiritual impurities. Mary Magdalene anointed the feet of Jesus with spikenard oil. All through ancient history, aromatic oils were used as medicines, cosmetics, and tools to heighten spirituality.

Scent takes us to the depths of sensuality and passion. It awakens lost parts of our souls through the intimate connection of smell and our primal being. We can travel through memories of our existence with odoriferous cues. Aromatherapy brings us in intimate contact with nature. It allows us to share part of the plant world known by bees and butterflies. When we are privileged to use medicines the earth provides, we see the perfection of nature—we can be healed by the simplest of nature's remedies. Yet the exact action of many of nature's cures is still a mystery to our supposedly sophisticated science.

In the following pages, you will learn what essential oils are, where they come from, and how to use them to enhance the total health and well-being of yourself and your loved ones. You will witness the evolution of aromatherapy throughout history and learn how modern research is playing a role in validating the traditional use of aromatherapy and botanical medicine. With the guidance to be found in this book, you can effectively incorporate aromatherapy into your everyday life.

1

An Introduction to Aromatherapy

One of my reasons for writing this book is to remove misconceptions and offer accurate information on the science and art of aromatherapy. When I first became involved with aromatherapy, only two books on the topic were available: Jean Valnet's *The Practice of Aromatherapy* and Robert Tisserand's *The Art of Aromatherapy*. Since that time, many books have been written on the subject, many by lay writers who are not practicing aromatherapists. These writers have little experience with the vast clinical uses of essential oils. The result is that only a superficial knowledge of aromatherapy has been made available to readers and many of the broader benefits have not been represented. The media and the cosmetics industry have trivialized aromatherapy, portraying it simply as the use of pleasant smells to make face creams and bath products more enjoyable. In contrast,

European countries such as France and England hold aromatherapy in great respect as a natural medical therapy.

When I first began on my path in the healing arts, training in aromatherapy was not available in the United States, so I went to England to study with Shirley Price. My studies then led me to explore the medical aspects of aromatherapy, studying under French medical aromatherapists Dr. Jean-Claude Lapraz, Pierre Franchome, and Jean-Michele Salette, who taught me the importance of aromatherapy in treating a broad range of medical conditions, especially infectious disease. I delved into working with the body's elimination pathways, primarily the lymphatic system, as well as the effect of aromatics on the mind.

New scientific research continually validates aromatherapy's health-giving benefits. Once we come to an authentic understanding of available treatments using essential oils, we can reap the multitude of benefits this dynamic holistic therapy has to offer.

WHAT IS AROMATHERAPY?

Aromatherapy is the therapeutic use of essential oils for health and well-being. The name *aromatherapy* in itself is somewhat misleading: Scent is only one aspect of aromatherapy. Aroma and olfaction are important parts of the therapy and are useful for treatment of psychological conditions, but, as you will learn in this book, aromatherapy is used in many different ways.

A branch of botanical medicine, aromatherapy is a plant-based therapy. Essential oils are extracted from oil sacs in flowers, leaves, roots, seeds, woods, and bark. To be utilized in the form we recognize as essential oils, these plant oils must be extracted using specialized distillation methods. The result is a highly concentrated, fragrant oil, rich in chemical compounds. The aromatic compounds contained in essential oils have many potent medicinal benefits, including antibacterial, antimicrobial, and antiviral properties.

The quality of essential oils has a great effect on the therapeutic results. The methods of distillation and growing conditions both have an impact on the quality of essential oils. Commercial aromatherapy products often contain inferior essential oils or even synthetic fragrance oils. For aromatherapy to truly benefit health, only pure, high-quality essential oils must be used.

3

THE BENEFITS OF AROMATHERAPY

To market a pharmaceutical drug, a company first typically spends $500 million in research. In light of the rising expense of drugs, aromatherapy is economical. Although some essential oils, such as rose, are costly, only a few drops are needed to make an aromatherapy blend. It may not be feasible to totally replace traditional drug treatments with aromatherapy, but it is possible to lessen dosages in many cases. Anxiety-related conditions respond to chamomile and clary sage. Arthritis sufferers can use lavender to reduce pain and inflammation. Incorporating aromatherapy and other natural therapies into a medical care regime allows the care of chronic conditions to be less drug-oriented and leaves the conventional medical community more time and resources to devote to emergency care and care of severe conditions.

Aromatherapy is unique in its ease of use and diverse methods of application. Essential oils can enter the body through inhalation, bathing, topical application, and internal (oral) use. These varied methods of application make aromatherapy an efficient way to treat localized conditions that are otherwise difficult to cure. Topical application of essential oils is ideal for treatment of wounds. For certain infectious conditions and digestive disorders, essential oils can be taken internally. Sinus infections that are difficult to treat respond well to oil of eucalyptus used in vapor form.

Aromatherapy can also take the form of a massage treatment. The small molecular size of essential oils allows them to penetrate deep into the body, allowing the healing power to work on an internal level and affecting overall health. The aromas act on the nervous system during a massage treatment, reducing the tension that is at the root of many conditions. Stress disorders respond profoundly to aromatherapy massage.

The mind, spirit, and psyche are uplifted through scent. Through our olfactory process, aromas act on brain chemistry. Studies have shown essential oils have a marked effect on the limbic system, the part of the brain that controls emotion. For emotional health, essential oils can be diffused into the air or worn as fragrance. They can be applied to the pulse points so the scent surrounds and comforts throughout the day. Aromatherapy is useful in balancing psychological conditions such as depression, anxiety, and mental fatigue, as well as contributing to general mood enhancement and stress reduction.

For women's disorders, aromatherapy can take the form of suppositories, douches, sitz baths, and local external application.

Conditions such as PMS, menstrual cramps, menopause, pregnancy, bladder infections, and vaginal infections all respond well to aromatherapy. As a preventive medicine, aromatherapy is unsurpassed. Essential oils dispersed into the atmosphere from a diffuser can kill harmful bacteria and microorganisms before they invade the body, guarding against infection. Aromatherapy aids in elimination of toxic waste through its action on the lymphatic system, circulation, liver, and kidneys. Some essential oils are sudorific—that is, they eliminate waste by inducing sweat. Essential oils are also immune-system stimulants, increasing the process of phagocytosis (the destruction of invading microorganisms by white blood cells).

5

Aromatherapy increases circulation and oxygenation in the skin, making it an ideal beauty therapy. Essential oils rejuvenate the skin and slow the aging process. Aromatherapy can take the form of face masks, steams, and topical oil blends. Skin disorders such as acne can be treated with topical application of tea tree oil. Studies have shown it cures acne as effectively as conventional benzoyl peroxide treatment, without side effects or irritation.

In my years of practice as a clinical aromatherapist and medical herbalist, I have found the versatility of aromatherapy adds a new dimension to healing. Essential oils are able to affect many levels of the body's system from the simple application of an aromatherapy blend. I have seen many successful cases in which health was restored by using aromatherapy. I now consider essential oils my treatment of choice for many conditions. *Calophyllum inophyllum* and *Ravensara aromatica* are effective against herpes zoster (shingles). *Thymus vulgaris* and *Eucalyptus radiata* are very effective for respiratory infection when used top-ically or in a steam inhalation. *Melaleuca alternifolia* (tea tree oil) is effective against candida infections.

I have treated many cases of human papilloma virus (HPV—venereal warts) with successful results. Genital herpes (herpes simplex 2) outbreaks can be prevented (although not cured) with a particular blend that includes tea tree oil. Many her-pes sufferers report that the frequency of outbreaks is dramatically reduced after using aromatherapy. Cold sores (herpes simplex 1) are quickly alleviated with application of melissa essential oil.

One very special experience I had early in my practice was treating a case of rectal cancer that had not responded to con-ventional medical treatment. The cancerous tumor had been sur-gically removed and treated with conventional drugs. Within a few weeks of surgery, the tumor began to grow again, this time even larger. The case seemed hopeless. In researching the condi-tion, I discovered an oil that had been researched and found to be effective against rectal cancer in Japanese medical trials. Upon application of the oil mixture, the external tumor shrunk by 90 percent in twenty-four hours! This result, to my skeptical mind, was astounding and instilled in me great faith in the power of aromatherapy to heal.

Of course, the many everyday uses for aromatherapy are not so miraculous, but are infinitely beneficial. Small wonders, such as healing my new baby's diaper rash with geranium oil or treating viruses, are aromatherapy's most useful purpose. Using essential oils is a pleasant way to treat children without the dis-tress of forcing down oral over-the-counter cold medications. One of my own fondest childhood memories is of my mother massaging warm camphor oil on my chest when I was ill—an old home remedy that is in fact a form of aromatherapy. Indeed, I sometimes faked getting sick just to enjoy the warmth of her hands and the piercing smell of camphor.

Aromatherapy is a precious gift of nature with many health-giving benefits. Self-nurturing and caring for one's family with aromatherapy warm the heart and create memories that bond us together.

A BRIEF HISTORY OF AROMATHERAPY

Our senses instinctively distinguish foul smells as harmful and pleasant aromas as beneficial. The enticing scents of the aromatic plants may have led early humans to select these plants. Through trial and error, people discovered which plants were useful for food, spices, spiritual ritual, beautification of the body, and healing.

The oldest form of medicine in the world, ayurveda (Sanskrit for "science of life") dates back five thousand years in India. The vast diversity of plant life, including fennel, turmeric, long pepper, sandalwood, ashwagandha, garlic, cardamom, cumin, clove, lemongrass, holy basil, chaulmoogra, khus khus (vetiver), patchouli, spikenard, benzoin, frankincense, and jasmine, led to the incorporation of aromatics into ayurvedic medicine. This richness of botanical resources also led to the export of many aromatic and medicinal herbs and spices, and with this trade came the exchange of knowledge. The medicine of India influenced much of the ancient world as ayurvedic concepts traveled throughout Southeast Asia and China.

The ancient Chinese pharmacy included two thousand primarily botanical substances. Some of these plant medicines are still used today in pharmaceutical drugs, such as the ephedrine found in hayfever medications, which comes from the Chinese plant ma-huang.

Herbal medicine was also highly developed in Egypt, where official schools of herbalism are believed to have existed as early as 3000 B.C. One of Egypt's earliest medical texts, known today as the Ebers Papyrus, contains recipes for salves, ointments, decoctions, and various herbal preparations brewed with wine, as well as more than seven hundred medicinal herbs, many of which are aromatic plants. Aromatic botanicals used by the Egyptians included myrrh, peppermint, cinnamon, wormwood, aniseed, frankincense, galbanum, juniper, fir, cypress, black pepper, fennel, cumin, marjoram, onion, garlic, and asafoetida.

Hippocrates, the Greek healer often called "the father of medicine," derived much of his knowledge of medicine from the Egyptians. His principles were similar to those of today's holistic medicine in that he held diet, sunshine, and pure water to be important factors in maintaining good health. He also understood the antibacterial properties of aromatic plants: During an epidemic of plague, he urged the people of Athens to burn aromatic plants to prevent the spread of the disease.

The first treatise on what we now consider aromatherapy, *Concerning Odors*, was written by the Greek Theophrastus (372–285 B.C.), who was perhaps the first scientific botanist. He discussed the effect of fragrance on the mind, observing for the first time the connection between taste and olfaction (smell).

8

Perhaps the most important event in the development of modern aromatherapy was the extraction of plants' volatile compounds by steam distillation—the creation of essential oils. Crude forms of distillation appear to have existed as early as 3500 B.C., but it was not until Persian philosopher and healer Avicenna (980–1037 A.D.) first distilled rose essence that the science of essential oil distillation as we know it today was created. Soon after Avicenna's discovery, essential oil of rose and rose floral waters became sought-after exports from Arabia. European perfumers incorporated essential oils into their fragrances. By the mid-1500s, many aromatic botanicals were being distilled for essential oils, including pine, frankincense, saffron, labdanum, carrot seed, fennel, nutmeg, rue, cloves, marjoram, ginger, cardamom, thyme, and asafoetida.

9

As time went on, essential oils began to be used widely as medicines. Rene-Maurice Gattefosse, a French chemist, coined the term *aromatherapy* and wrote the first book on modern-day aromatherapy in 1937. Gattefosse had discovered that essential oils were more antiseptic than the chemical antiseptics in use at the time. When his hand was badly burned in a laboratory accident, he immediately immersed it in lavender oil. To his astonishment, the burn healed rapidly, without infection or scarring. During World War II, French doctor Jean Valnet treated battle wounds with essential oils and used the knowledge he gained during the war to develop aromatherapy into the modern medical treatment we know today.

Today, forward-thinking researchers continue to explore the medicinal uses of essential oils. Pierre Franchome of France has studied the efficacy of essential oils against infectious diseases; Dr. Kurt Schnaubelt has examined the chemical nature of essential oil components and the ways these components function as medicinal substances. Practicing aromatherapists can obtain certification in schools accredited by self-regulated organizations. Aromatherapy is a rapidly growing, increasingly recognized holistic healing practice. In the following chapters, we'll look at the ways aromatherapy can heal.

2

How Aromatherapy Works

SCENT AND THE MIND

Olfaction is the process of the brain perceiving odor—of smelling. Aromatic molecules are inhaled into the nasal passages, where they come in contact with the olfactory epithelium, a small, dime-sized area in the nasal cavities behind the bridge of the nose. The mucous layer of the epithelium is covered with receptor-bearing cilia, which are like little antennas attached to neurons, or nerve cells. The various shapes of the aromatic molecules fit together with these receptors like a lock and key. Twenty million olfactory neurons receive and transmit information to the olfactory bulb. (These unique neurons are the only nerve cells in our system that can both transmit and receive information, as well as regenerate themselves.) The olfactory nerves then carry the odor messages to the part of the brain called the limbic system.

Smell is the only sense that goes directly to the limbic system, bypassing the cerebral cortex, the intellectual part of the brain. Other senses such as sight and hearing must register with the cortex before entering other parts of the brain. In other words, our sense of smell is our only direct link from the outer world to our inner world.

The limbic system is the center of memory and emotion. Scent can provoke powerful and primal feelings in all living beings. We have all experienced strong emotions or recalled a particular memory upon smelling a scent connected to events in our lives. Aromas can enhance memory retention. When a group of schoolchildren were given a list of words to memorize, some were given an aroma to smell along with the words. The children who smelled the aroma had better memory retention and were better able to recall the list than the children who did not smell the aroma.

From the limbic system, odor messages go to the hypothalamus, which sends messages to other parts of the brain. When the brain receives odor stimulation, it releases various neurotransmitters. Each area of the brain releases a different type of neurotransmitter. The thalamus releases enkephalins, which kill pain, induce euphoria, and promote a feeling of well-being. The raphe nucleus releases serotonin, which promotes relaxation and sleep. The pituitary gland releases endorphins, which kill pain, promote euphoria, and may stimulate sexual feelings. The locus ceruleus releases noradrenaline, which is a stimulant that keeps us alert and awake.

Odor messages are one of the fastest ways to achieve psychological or physiological effects. Through the connection between the limbic system and other parts of the brain, many functions of the body and mind may be regulated by smell, such as hormone balance, breathing, heart rate, blood pressure, stress levels, and memory.

ESSENTIAL OILS TO BALANCE YOUR EMOTIONS AND YOUR MIND

CONDITION	ESSENTIAL OILS
Poor memory, difficulty concentrating, fatigue	Basil, rosemary, peppermint, lemon
Lack of confidence, sexual problems (e.g., frigidity, impotence)	Ylang-ylang, jasmine, clary sage
Insomnia, stress, anxiety, high blood pressure	Marjoram, neroli, lavender, chamomile
Sluggish immunity, boredom, the need for stimulation	Juniper, cardamom, rosemary, lemongrass
Depression, mood swings	Clary sage, grapefruit, rose, jasmine
Sadness, grief	Neroli, melissa, rose
Fear	Frankincense, cedarwood

13

Scent and Sexuality

Sexuality and scent in particular are closely linked. Indeed, anosmia (loss of the ability to smell) diminishes libido in one-fourth of its sufferers. Studies have suggested that women may choose a mate according to scent. Odor carries genetic messages regarding immunity; a mate may be chosen because his odor indicates that his immunity will enhance that of the offspring. Birth-control pills diminish a women's ability to detect these odor messages, so a woman going off the pill may find she is no longer as pleased with her choice in mates! In one study, apocrine scent excreted from the male axillary (armpit) was sprayed on chairs in a waiting room. Women chose to sit in the apocrine-scented chairs more often than the unscented chairs, even though the scent was not detectable at conscious levels. In other studies, men who were isolated from the scent of women grew less facial hair. Women kept in olfactory isolation from men had longer menstrual cycles than usual, but when brought in contact with men at least three times a week, their menstrual cycles shortened, indicating that they ovulated more frequently in response to the presence of men.

Human odor attraction seems to work like this: During a woman's most fertile periods, her scent is the strongest and most alluring. In response to her odor, the man produces odor to the degree of his arousal. His scent in turn acts as an aphrodisiac to the woman.

ABSORPTION INTO
THE CIRCULATORY SYSTEM

Essential oils are oil soluble and of low molecular weight, and are therefore able to mix with the sebaceous (oil) secretions of the skin. The skin was once thought to be an impenetrable barrier, but we now know certain substances have the ability to penetrate skin (e.g., pharmaceutical drugs are commonly administered dermally, in the form of a skin patch). Essential oils readily penetrate the skin's sebaceous glands, travel into the lower layers of the skin, and enter the bloodstream through the capillary system. This process takes about twenty minutes. You can see for yourself the skin's ability to absorb odor molecules: Place a cut clove of garlic on the soles of your feet. In a few hours, the smell of garlic will be on your breath.

The skin is an organ of both absorption and elimination. This makes skin massage an ideal vehicle for aromatherapy. Each essential oil has unique medicinal properties and an affinity for a particular system of the body. When applied to the skin, the essential oil can travel through the circulatory system and bring its therapeutic effects to the needy area. Essential oils can also help in the elimination of toxins by strengthening the lymphatic system, the body's primary waste-disposal system.

15

3

What Are Essential Oils?

Essential oils come from the roots, leaves, flowers, fruits, stems, bark, wood, and seeds of aromatic plants. They are contained in special oil sacs in the plant and are concentrated in various parts of the plant. Volatile, aromatic molecules composed of complex chemical constituents comprise essential oils. *Volatile* means that the aromatic molecules will evaporate and become airborne upon contact with the atmosphere or with heat. (It also means that they are flammable.) Being volatile, these molecules tend to evaporate from plants in the heat of the day and concentrate in the cool of night. This is why the time of day a plant is picked for distillation is most important in regard to its yield.

In the lives of plants, essential oils have several specialized purposes. They give flavor and fragrance to plants, which encourages pollination by insects and may protect the plant from moisture loss. Some essential oils are toxic. They contain chemicals that repel the microorganisms that may infect the plant or insects and animals that feed on the plant.

The purpose for which nature intended a particular plant aromatic often correlates with its use in aromatherapy. For example, jasmine has an intoxicating aroma that attracts pollinators as part of its reproductive cycle. In aromatherapy, jasmine is used for frigidity and reproductive problems. The herb wormwood, as its name indicates, has traditionally been used as a vermifuge (a substance that kills internal parasites and worms in humans). The toxic essential oil of wormwood serves the same purpose in the plant, protecting it from parasites.

18

EXTRACTION METHODS

The essential oil of aromatic plant parts is extracted by various methods, but the most widely used method today is steam distillation.

Steam Distillation

In steam distillation, plant material is placed in a still. Water is heated in another vessel and steam is sent through a coil into the still. As vapor passes through the plant material, the essential oil molecules vaporize and are released from the plant. The essential oil–saturated vapor rises out through refrigerated tubing, where it condenses and is drained off. Steam distillation allows for rapid processing, preserving delicate constituents such as esters (see page 21). For plants that have heat-sensitive components, distillation can also be performed at low temperatures. These sophisticated methods can be customized to create highly concentrated, fragrant oils rich in chemical compounds, which are sought after by knowledgeable aromatherapists.

In traditional distillation, water and plant material are both placed in the still and heated. The essential oils are carried by the steam through a gooseneck tube that leads into a receptacle. The receptacle contains water; because most essential oils are lighter than water, the oil floats to the top and is drained off. This method is commonly used for "on location" or "in the field" essential oil distillation.

The leftover water from this process, called a hydrosol, is also of gentle therapeutic value. The hydrosol contains water-soluble, nonvolatile plant extracts that can be used internally or for children's ailments.

The metal of the still has a great effect on the quality of the oil produced. (See pages 22–27 for more on quality and purity.) Steel is best, because it does not react with the plant chemicals. Aluminum can contaminate the essential oil because it reacts with phenols, contained in thyme and wintergreen. Wooden stills are economical and do not affect the oil adversely, but they retain the odor of the plant and so can only be used to distill one type of plant.

Enfleurage

The enfleurage method was traditionally used for highly fragrant flowers, such as jasmine, whose scent is too delicate to be extracted by steam. In this method, fat is spread on sheets of glass.

19

The flowers are then pressed into the layer of fat. Every two days, new flowers are added, until the fat is saturated with essential oil. The result of this process, which may take weeks, is a concentrated fragrant unguent. Alcohol is then used to separate the essential oil from the fat. This method, used since ancient times, is rarely used today, because it is inefficient, uneconomical, and time-consuming.

Cold-Pressing

Cold-pressing is exclusively used for citrus fruits. Essential oils are contained in glands in the rinds of lemons, oranges, and limes. The rinds are chopped and mixed with water; then pressure is applied to extract the oil. No heat is used, as it deteriorates the oil. Only organically grown fruit should be used because otherwise the residue of pesticides will remain in the essential oil, making the oil inappropriate for aromatherapy.

Solvent Extraction

Solvent extraction is a chemical process using petroleum ether (isomeric hexane). (Benzene, another solvent, is no longer used to extract essential oils because it is carcinogenic.) Aromatics extracted with this method are called absolutes. In general, solvent-extracted absolutes are not used in aromatherapy, with the exception of certain aromatics, such as hexane-processed jasmine.

In solvent extraction, the blossoms are placed in a hermetically sealed container through which the solvent is percolated. This results in a waxlike substance called a concrete. The essential oil is then separated from the concrete with a process using ethyl alcohol. The alcohol is removed by a final distillation process. Only very delicate florals such as violet, jasmine, hyacinth, Spanish broom, oakmoss, carnation, and boronia are extracted with this very costly method.

CHEMISTRY OF ESSENTIAL OILS

Essential oils are complex cocktails of carbon, hydrogen, and oxygen—the basic building blocks of life. Aromatic molecules are primarily divided into two chemical groups: terpenes and phenylpropane derivatives. The terpenes are divided into the subgroups monoterpenes, sesquiterpenes, diterpenes, and triterpenes. These groups can be further subdivided into the primary types of aromatic components.

21

Monoterpenes

Ketones, found in the essential oils of sage and hyssop, are mucolytic (they dissolve and loosen mucus congestion). They are also fat-soluble and cicatrizing (they help regenerate skin tissue) and can be toxic to the nervous system.

Esters, found in clary sage and lavender, relax the nervous system and are antispasmodic, fungicidal, anti-inflammative, and calming to the skin.

Aldehydes, found in melissa and citronella, are calming to the nervous system, anti-inflammative, antiviral, hypotensors, and antipyretic.

Alcohols, found in peppermint, coriander, and palmarosa, are tonic, stimulating, antibacterial, and antiviral and are generally safe and nontoxic.

Monoterpenes, found in orange and pine, are stimulants and antiseptic and may cause irritation.

Phenols, found in oregano and thyme, are stimulants, strong bactericides, and immunostimulants. They can also be irritants.

Oxides, found in tea tree, eucalyptus, and niaouli, are expectorant and mucolytic and can be skin irritants.

Sesquiterpenes

Lactones, found in laurel and *Inula graveolens*, are mucolytic and immunostimulant. Some essential oils of this group contain coumarins, which are anticoagulant.

Sesquiterpene-hydrocarbons, found in German chamomile, are anti-inflammative, antiviral, and soothing.

Phenylpropanes

Estragoles, found in tarragon and basil, are antispasmodic.

Cinnamic aldehydes, found in clove and cinnamon, are antiseptic and strongly fungicidal. Clove, traditionally used in dentistry, is anesthetic and may inhibit certain carcinogenic processes.

BUYING ESSENTIAL OILS

There are currently no regulations regarding the quality and purity of essential oils sold in the United States. (This is in stark contrast to France, where essential oils are sold by pharmacists and prescribed by medical doctors.) It is important to understand the principles of quality so you can make an educated choice when buying essential oils. The therapeutic benefits of aromatherapy can only be fully received if the essential oils are of good quality and are used properly and safely.

Despite the recent resurgence of aromatherapy, modern essential oils still are primarily manufactured as perfume and flavoring agents. The criteria of the perfume industry are far different from those of an aromatherapist. Even the finest perfume oils may not be suitable for therapeutic use. Many perfume essences are extracted with chemical solvents, because this mode of extraction yields the most potent scent. Small amounts of solvent impurities are left in the oil, making solvent-extracted essences unsuitable for aromatherapy purposes.

Quality of Extraction Methods

Distilled essential oils are the primary aromatics of choice for aromatherapy. Distilled oils, however, vary greatly in quality. Oils are adulterated in numerous ways undetectable to the untrained nose. "Doctoring the sauce" is a common practice of commercial manufacturers. Essential oils are extended with vegetable oil, mineral oil, or alcohol. Synthetic constituents are added to make the oil more marketable. For instance, to extend costly rose oil, a constituent such as synthetic geraniol will be added. These mixtures of synthetic aromas and natural essential oils are often sold as pure essential oils. Besides synthetics, natural essential oils are also blended with other essential oils (e.g., yarrow may be added to chamomile, lemongrass to lemon). The more costly the oil, the more common the practice of adulteration.

Another common practice is to rectify essential oils by redistillation, thereby increasing a desired constituent and removing undesired components such as terpenes. However, rectified or deterpenated oils are not suitable for aromatherapy purposes, which require complete oils. Complete oils buffer users from chemical compounds contained in the oil, which in their isolated state might cause harmful and allergic reactions. This kind of adulteration accounts for many of the cases of allergic reactions to oils.

Specialized distillation methods are used for essential oils intended for therapeutic use. One such method is water steam distillation, keeping the temperature lower than the lowest boiling point of the essential oil within the plant material being distilled. This low temperature preserves the integrity of the essential oil and some of the more volatile compounds in the oil sacs of the plant material.

Cold-pressing, an excellent method for extracting oils, is used only for the Rutaceae (citrus) family of oils. Citrus oils such as bergamot are technically not essential oils but essences, because they contain natural pigments. Citrus oils prepared for commercial use are deterpenated, making them inappropriate for aromatherapy.

Each species of plant must be distilled for a different length of time in order to extract all the chemical components. This is very important in aromatherapy, because it is the synergy of the plant's essence that does the job: The main constituents are no less important than the minuscule constituents. This synergy enables essential oils to work on many levels simultaneously. Incomplete oils do not have this depth of physiological action. In *Rosa dam-*

ascena (rose oil), for instance, minuscule constituents that account for less than 1 percent of the total are essential in composing the fragrance and creating the medicinal action of the oil.

Length of distillation time greatly affects the quality of oil yielded. The different grades of ylang (*Cananga odorata*) are an example. Ylang-ylang extra, the finest grade, is distilled for as little as twenty minutes. Ylang-ylang one, also good quality, is distilled for two hours. The lesser grades two and three are distilled up to twenty-four hours and have a chemical profile totally different from that of the first two grades.

Quality of the Plants Used

Essential oils are much like wine in that their quality and character varies from one growing season to the next. Plants should be harvested by experienced and knowledgeable pickers. The time of year, time of day, and whether the plant is in bloom all affect the final product.

For example, clary sage should be picked after flowering at the time of seeding. Lavender in flower should be cut before morning dew with a sickle by hand; machine-cut lavender yields a lesser-quality oil. The plants should be distilled as soon as possible, preferably at the same locale in which they were grown. Many high-quality plants are grown and distilled, for instance, in Grasse, France. In fact, the area's name derives from its reputation for oils—*grasse* translates to "grease" or "oil."

Farming practices and growing conditions, including quality of soil, all have a great bearing on the resulting essential oil. Wild plants yield essential oils with great character. For example, lavender that grows wild at high altitudes will have a higher content of esters, a relaxing component. Oils for aromatherapy purposes should be grown organically, without chemical fertilizers or pesticides, which are oil-soluble and will remain in the final product.

Each type of plant has conditions and climate that ideally suit its needs. Thus, the country of origin is also a factor of quality. The region of Mysore in India, for instance, grows the best sandalwood. Different climates and habitats yield oils with varying therapeutic properties.

Botanical Names

26

Knowing the plant's botanical name is helpful when looking for a particular oil. For instance, a hybrid lavender called lavandin is widely sold as commercial lavender oil, although it does not have the same properties as *Lavandula officinalis* (true lavender). *Eucalyptus radiata* does not have the same therapeutic effect as *Eucalyptus globulus*.

Be aware that there is much confusion about the botanical names of certain species. For example, sweet marjoram has the botanical name *Origanum majorana*, but it is also called *Majorana hortensis*. Sometimes it is confused with Spanish origanum or Spanish marjoram, which are actually both thymes and have different properties.

The chemical components of essential oils each have a unique physiological effect when used in therapy (see "Chemistry of Essential Oils," pages 21–22). Gas chromatograph analysis can verify much of the quality and purity of essential oils and enable aromatherapists to set standardized chemotypes for specific botanical species of essential oils.

The integrity of essential oils is the absolute heart of aromatherapy. For oils to be pure, natural, and complete, they should contain no adulterants or additives and should not have been rendered incomplete by deterpenation and redistillation. Essential oils for aromatherapy should be distilled from plants grown wild or organically cultivated. They should be identified as specific botanical species and extracted with proper distillation methods. Unfortunately, aromatic botanicals that meet these criteria are almost unavailable commercially. One of the telling signs is the low price of aromatic oils available in retail stores. Quality essential oils are expensive (although high price is not necessarily a guarantee of high quality).

Until high standards and quality control become the norm, how do we choose the right essential oils? Try to find a dealer who is knowledgeable in aromatherapy. Perhaps there is a certified aromatherapist in your area who sells aromatherapy products. Ask questions: Have all the criteria been met? Does the distributor test the oils with gas chromatography? Is literature provided that guarantees specific standards have been met?

Train your nose. By smelling many oils, you will eventually be able to detect simple adulterants such as alcohol. Pour a drop of essential oil on a piece of clean white paper. Pure essential oils will evaporate without a trace. If mineral oil or vegetable oil have been added, a stain will be left. Knowledgeable consumers will create a demand for high-quality essential oils and enhance the benefits we all receive from this truly holistic therapy.

4

How to Use Essential Oils

BLENDING WITH CARRIERS

Essential oils are generally not used undiluted. Large quantities of plant material are needed to extract a small quantity of essential oil, creating a highly concentrated substance. For example, 5,000 pounds of rose petals are required to make 1 pound of essential oil. Essential oils are often too strong to use alone, so it is necessary to blend the essential oils with other substances called carriers. Carriers are the base substances used to carry and disperse a small quantity of essential oils onto a larger area of the skin or into the body. Substances used as carriers include vinegar, wine, alcohol, water, milk, egg yolk, and white lotion, but the most common carrier method is to blend the essential oil with a vegetable or seed oil.

Ratios of Essential Oils to Carriers

The standard dilution of essential oil in a carrier is 2 percent to 2.5 percent (for adults). For example, 15 drops of essential oil in 1 ounce (30 milliliters) of carrier is a 2.5 percent dilution.

MAKING A CARRIER FORMULA

ESSENTIAL OIL	CARRIER
40 to 60 drops	4 ounces (120 mililiters)
25 to 30 drops	2 ounces (50 mililiters)
10 to 15 drops	1 ounce (30 mililiters)
5 to 7 drops	½ ounce (15 mililiters)
4 to 10 drops	2 teaspoons (10 mililiters)
2 to 5 drops	1 teaspoon (5 mililiters)

30

Carrier Oils

Carriers oils are always natural oils of vegetable origin, sometimes called fixed oils because they are not volatile (do not evaporate) or fatty oils because of their lipid content. Essential oils readily mix with oil. Synthetics and petroleum-based mineral oils are never suitable for aromatherapeutic use.

Oils of vegetable origin are therapeutic substances themselves. Many vegetable oils and nut oils, such as wheat germ and

Measurements Used in Aromatherapy

25 milligrams equals 1 drop

5 milliliters (100 drops) equals 1 teaspoon

15 milliliters equals ½ ounce or 1 tablespoon

30 milliliters equals 1 ounce

1,000 milliliters (1 liter) equals 1.76 pints

1 cup equals 8 ounces

1 ounce equals 28.35 grams

1 gram equals 1 milliliter

1 milliliter equals 20 drops

1 squirt of a standard-size eye dropper is approximately 20 to 25 drops, which equals approximately 1 milliliter. Eye droppers with milliliter measures are sold at pharmacies.

31

hazelnut, contain antioxidants like vitamin E. Antioxidants protect the integrity of cell membranes, which are composed of lipids (fats). Lipids can be damaged by free radicals (oxidation), which can harden the membrane wall, hindering the absorption of the nutrients necessary for the life of the cell.

When purchasing vegetable oils to make aromatherapy formulas, look for natural oil made from organically grown plants without additives.

Apricot Kernel
Rich in vitamins and fatty acids such as gamma linolenic acids (GLA). Essential fatty acids such as GLA are important in many

bodily functions, such as the anti-inflammatory process. Apricot kernel oil is indicated for devitalized or wrinkled skin.

Avocado

Rich in vitamins A and D. One kilogram of oil contains approximately 20,000 units of vitamin A and 40,000 units of vitamin D. It also includes the nutrients vitamins B_1, B_2, D, and E, pantothenic acid, lecithin, and fatty acids. This oil contains unsaponifiable substances (substances that can't decompose into acid, salt, or alcohol). These unsaponifiable substances have many healing benefits, including softening hardened tissues that have lost their elasticity as well as accelerating the wound-healing process. Avocado oil is indicated for cellulite conditions and hair loss.

Grapeseed

Contains minerals, vitamins, proteins, and linoleic acid. This oil is light and cholesterol-free with good skin penetration. Suitable for all skin types, especially oily skin.

Hazelnut

Contains minerals, vitamins, and the essential fatty acids linoleic acid and oleic acid. Absorbed into the skin quickly. Has a tonifying and astringent action on the skin. Good for dry, devitalized, or sun-damaged skin.

Rosehip Seed (Rosa aff. rubiginosa, Rosa mosqueta)

Contains gamma linoleic acid, linolenic acids, palmitic acid, vitamin C, and pectin. Rosehip oil heals many conditions, including burns, all types of scars (including scars from radiation treatment), hyperpigmentation, sun-damaged skin and hair, eczema, psoriasis, ulcerated veins, and skin ulcers. Regenerates prematurely aged skin. Indicated for dry and devitalized skin.

Macadamia Nut

Contains 18 percent palmitoleic acid, 60 percent oleic acid, and 6 percent linoleic/linolenic fatty acids. Palmitoleic acid is found in human sebum (a fatty lubricant substance secreted by sebaceous glands of the skin) and in large amounts in the skin oils of children. Palmitoleic acid is protective, and it appears to slow the aging process. This oil is very stable and resistant to rancidity. It tonifies sagging tissues and moisturizes dry skin. It is suitable for all skin types.

33

Sesame Oil

Contains minerals, proteins, vitamin E, and lecithin. An important oil in ayurvedic medicine used to pacify the *vata* constitution, one of the three ayurvedic constitutional types, which tends to have a small-boned, lean physique and a sensitive, nervous temperament and is prone to constipation, dyspepsia, insomnia, anxiety, and dry skin (see page 71). Sesame oil is nourishing and softening. It is beneficial for treating eczema, psoriasis, rheumatic conditions, and tanning. Indicated for all skin types.

Sunflower Oil

Contains unsaturated fatty acids, vitamins A, B, D, and E, minerals, and lecithin. Ayurvedic medicine uses sunflower oil to treat *pitta* (conditions of excess heat) disorders. Sunflower oil helps prevent skin conditions from occurring. It is beneficial for most diseases of the skin, bruises, diaper rash, cradle cap, and leg ulcers. Indicated for all skin types.

Wheat Germ

Contains vitamins A, D, and E, essential fatty acids, lecithin, protein, sterols, and minerals. Wheat germ oil is an excellent source of vitamin E, which protects skin fats from decomposition from oxygen through its antioxidant properties. Added to formulas, wheat germ oil supports skin regeneration and aids in muscle and lymph function. It preserves the shelf life of aromatherapy blends. It is beneficial for eczema, psoriasis, stretch marks, and premature aging. Indicated for dry, sensitive, and devitalized skin.

Herbal Oils

Herbal oils are extracts of medicinal plants. The constituents of the herbs are extracted by maceration (i.e., steeping) in a vegetable oil base. These oils differ from essential oils in their chemical profile and because they are fatty, nonvolatile substances. They can be used as part of a formula and as a carrier of essential oils. Herbal oils have varied medicinal properties. They work in synergy with essential oils to enhance the therapeutic effect of a formula.

St. John's Wort (Hypericum)

Contains hypericin and hypericinlike substances, flavonoids, monoterpenes, proanthocyanidins, vitamin C, pectin, and choline. St. John's wort oil has long been known as an excellent wound

healer, partly due to its antibacterial activity against staphylococcus. It reduces inflammation and soothes nerves. The many medicinal uses for St. John's wort include treating sprains, injuries,
bruises, burns, eczema, lumbago, shingles, cold sores, sciatica, neuralgia, ulcers, and hemorrhoids. A lower-back massage using St.
John's wort oil has been helpful for bedwetting.

Used internally in the form of a tincture or extract, St.
John's wort has many therapeutic benefits. It is used for nervous
disorders such as depression, and it is antiviral. St. John's wort has
been found effective against the herpes group of viruses.
Although these viruses remain in the system permanently, the
extract, taken internally, and the oil, applied topically, can alleviate a breakout of herpes simplex 1 and 2 and shingles. Taken
internally, the extract has been used to treat Epstein-Barr virus
and cytomegalovirus and is helpful in preventing opportunistic
herpes group infections in HIV patients.

Caution: When used topically on skin exposed to the sun,
the hypericin contained in the oil may cause photosensitivity.

Calendula

Contains salicylic acid, carotenoids, and phytosterols. Calendula
oil speeds wound closing, stimulates new tissue formation, mildly
stimulates circulation, and quickly reduces inflammation. It has
antiseptic and antimicrobial properties. Calendula has traditionally been used to treat acne, burns, impetigo, eczema, swelling,
sunburn, chapped skin, inflamed mucous membranes, bedsores,
and abrasions. Mixed with St. John's wort oil in equal portions,
it aids the healing of bruises. Calendula is soothing, regenerative,
and toning to the skin.

Calophyllum Inophyllum

Contains saturated fatty acids, glycerides, coumarin derivatives, terpenic essences, and phosphoamino acids. Calophyllum is not an infused oil but an extract that contains both aromatic and fatty substances. It stimulates phagocytosis, a function of the immune system that cleans up unwanted debris. For this reason calophyllum is used for pus skin conditions. It is beneficial for conditions such as sciatica, ulcers, wounds, shingles, chemical burns, pain, neuritis from leprosy, and surgical wounds.

Caution: Use carefully on sensitive skin.

APPLICATIONS

Inhalation Methods

Aroma Lamps

Aroma lamps are made of ceramic, glass, or marble, with a candle to heat the oil and vaporize the aromatic molecules into the air. Depending on the size of the room and the intensity of odor desired, 5 to 15 drops of oil is sufficient.

An easy way to scent a room and freshen the air without the benefit of an aroma lamp is to put 1 to 3 drops of essential oil on a light bulb. The heat of the bulb will disperse the aroma. This is an especially convenient method to use in hotel rooms while traveling.

Diffuser

Diffusers are electric and generally have a setting that regulates the amount of aroma dispersed. They have a glass nebulizer, which emits a fine spray of aromatic molecules. A diffuser may be used like an aroma lamp to dispense fragrance into the environment. They are most appropriate for use during a respiratory illness or to disinfect the air of an office or waiting room. When ill, use 5 to 10 drops of the appropriate essential oil (see chapters 5, 6, and 7) and inhale close to the glass nebulizer for ten to twenty minutes.

Humidifier

If you have a cold, flu, or bronchial infection, a humidifier can help loosen mucus deposits in the respiratory tract. The use of essential oils with a humidifier disinfects the room and fights infection. Add 3 to 10 drops of essential oil to the water four to ten times a day.

37

Facial or Respiratory Steam

Facial steam is used to clear sinus congestion, respiratory ailments, or skin conditions. Add 5 to 7 drops to a bowl of hot water or to a pot of water on a low simmer. Cover your head with a towel, hold your face over the water, close your eyes, and deeply inhale the vapors. May be repeated every three or four hours as necessary.

Portable Inhalation

Apply 6 to 10 drops to a handkerchief and store in a plastic bag to preserve the aroma. As necessary, hold the handkerchief close to your nose and inhale. Use to disinfect your nasal passages while traveling on airplanes, or to relieve stress, anxiety, and motion sickness.

Sauna

Essential oils used in a sauna bath detoxify the system and cleanse the bronchial tubes. Add 1 to 5 drops to a cup of water, then pour the water onto the sauna rocks. Use caution as you pour it onto the hot rocks, because essential oils are flammable.

Topical Applications

Compress

A compress treatment can be hot or cold, depending on the condition. Acute inflammations that are red or hot should be treated with cold compresses, which should be replaced as soon as they begin to warm. Repeat the process several times or as long as is needed to reduce heat or swelling. For aches and pains that are chronic or for an injury that is past the acute stage, use a hot compress and reapply as soon as it begins to cool. To retain the heat, cover the compress with plastic and a towel. Repeat applications as necessary. To stimulate healing or circulation in a stagnant condition, use alternating hot and cold compress applications.

For both hot and cold compresses the steps are the same: Fill a bowl with either hot or iced cold water. Add 4 to 6 drops of the appropriate essential oil. Dip a flannel or cloth in the bowl, wring it out, and apply to the area. Repeat application as necessary. You may add more essential oils as needed.

Massage Oils, Topical Blends, and Anointing Scents

To make an aromatherapy blend for topical application or massage, follow the ratio guidelines on page 30. The standard dilution is 2 to 2.5 percent, although some experts recommend a stronger or weaker blend, depending on the condition. For topical use, you may apply the blend to a localized area—for instance, apply to the chest for a bronchial condition. Massage may be full body, or of the back, hand, or foot, according to your needs.

FRAGRANCE NOTES OF ESSENTIAL OILS

FRAGRANCE NOTES	ESSENTIAL OILS
Top notes	Basil, bergamot, clary sage, coriander, eucalyptus, grapefruit, laurel, lemon, mandarin, myrtle, niaouli, orange, petitgrain, tea tree, thyme, verbena, yarrow
Middle notes	Aniseed, black pepper, chamomile, cypress, fennel, geranium, hyssop, juniper, lavender, marjoram, melissa, peppermint, pine, ravensara, rosemary
Base notes	Benzoin, cedar, champaca, cinnamon, clove, frankincense, ginger, hyacinth, jasmine, myrrh, neroli, patchouli, rose, sandalwood, spikenard, tarragon, tuberose, vetiver, ylang-ylang

Blending for a fragrant effect is one dimension of aromatherapy formulation. Generally, three to five essential oils are used to make a formula. Perfumers have categorized scents by the evaporation rates of the essential oil, from light (top notes) to heavy (base notes). The light notes tend to be refreshing and uplifting; the base notes tend to be heavy and sensual. To make a pleasing, well-rounded scent, blend oils from each category—top notes, middle notes, and base notes. For instance, for an uplifting fragrance, choose neroli from the base notes, geranium from the middle notes, and mandarin from the top notes.

Anointing Fragrances

An anointing fragrance can be created using the same principles of perfumery notes. The blend may be made from the pure oil without the addition of a carrier oil. The scent can be used to support your desires or emotional needs. If you need a more confident attitude, formulate a blend using clary sage as the centerpiece and anoint your solar plexus (just below the sternum and ribcage). If you want romance, use ylang-ylang as your centerpiece oil and apply it to your pulse points, located behind the earlobes, on the inner side of the wrist, and at the back of the knees. Veins are close to the surface of the skin in these areas and warm the oil, giving off the attractant scent.

Clinical Formulas

Blending for a medical rather than a fragrant effect is another dimension of aromatherapy formulation. Medical formulations are blended to achieve the curative effect desired. For example, antifungal oils such as tea tree or oregano are appropriate to treat a toenail fungal infection and would be your centerpiece oils for a clinical formula. Refer to the sections on the systems of the body to blend oils according to their clinical properties.

Baths

Standard Bath

Aromatic baths are a form of hydrotherapy (water therapy), beneficial for aches and pains, muscle tension, skin disorders, stress, and emotional well-being. For an aromatherapy bath, fill the tub with water. (Do not add the essential oils while the water is still running or they will evaporate.) Just before you get in, add 5 to 12 drops of essential oils. Agitate the water to disperse the oils. Soak in the tub for twenty minutes. After your bath, lightly dry and massage your skin with an aromatherapy blend.

Sitz Baths

Sitz baths are appropriate for hemorrhoids, lower back pain, or female disorders such as cramps, menstrual disorders, Bartholin cysts, vaginitis, and for healing the perineum after childbirth. A sitz bath is also referred to as a "hip bath," because only the pelvic region is immersed in water. Fill a tub the size of a large baby bathtub with warm water. Add 6 to 10 drops of essential oil. Sit in the tub with your legs and feet outside the tub and soak for 20 minutes.

Foot Baths

Foot baths are a traditional remedy for many conditions. The many blood vessels in the feet are able to carry the herbal or aromatic remedy all over the body. For sinusitis, use a foot bath of yarrow tea (2 cups) or essential oil of eucalyptus. Swollen feet or ankles benefit from a cool foot bath with lavender. For varicose veins, soak feet in a tepid bath with lemon oil. As a rule, add 6 to 10 drops of essential oil to foot baths.

Neat

Essential oils are used neat—undiluted and straight out of the bottle—for certain therapeutic purposes. Neat application is generally reserved for spot treatment, such as lavender oil for insect bites or emergency treatment of burns.

Internal Use

Only therapeutic-grade essential oils should be taken internally. Use caution and seek the guidance of a qualified aromatherapist or medical professional before using essential oils internally. Refer to chapter 9 on safety and toxicity.

For internal use, place 1 or 2 drops of essential oil on one of the following base substances: a sugar cube, a spoonful of honey, a small piece of bread or charcoal, a tea bag, or in a tablespoon of wine or cup of tea. Dosage guidelines for internal use are 1 drop per 55.3 pounds (25 kilograms) of weight. Do not exceed 3 drops taken 3 times a day.

Essential oils should not be used internally for long periods of time. The length of treatment ranges from less than a week to ten days. Often only one or two doses are all that is necessary. The maximum length of time essential oils should be taken internally is three weeks.

DOSAGE FOR CHILDREN

When using essential oils for children, always check the safety of the oil first. Check the list of toxic oils on pages 126–127, and avoid all irritating, toxic, or strong essential oils. For children younger than thirteen, reduce the dosage to half the adult dosage, and continue to reduce by age and weight of the child. Young's formula is commonly used to determine the appropriate dosage:

Age in years / Age + 12 = Portion of adult dose

For example, the correct dose for a four-year-old child would be:

4 / 4 + 12 = 4 /16 = 1/4 of adult dose

Never give children essential oils internally. Do not use essential oils on newborns. Always keep essential oils out of reach of children.

DOSAGE FOR
THE FRAIL OR ELDERLY

In general, elderly people need less essential oil to produce a therapeutic response. Reduce the dosage according to the person's constitution. For example, the standard dilution for an adult is 7 to 15 drops per 1 ounce of carrier. If the elderly person has a strong constitution, use the higher dose of 15 drops; if the person is frail, use 7 drops so less essential oil penetrates the system per application.

43

STORAGE AND SHELF LIFE

Essential oils are volatile substances, which makes them sensitive to sunlight. Prolonged exposure can cause the essential oil to oxidize and lose potency. Store your aromatics in a cool dark place, such as inside a cabinet. Essential oils can interact with some plastics, so it is best to keep your aromatic blends or pure oils in amber glass bottles. (The amber color protects the oils from excess light exposure.) Most essential oils have a shelf life of about a year. Citrus oils lose their potency most quickly; heavy oils like patchouli are stable the longest.

Carrier oils also turn rancid over an extended period of time and deteriorate with excess exposure to sunlight and oxygen. Most carrier oils like wheat germ and hazelnut oil have a shelf life of eight to ten months. Store them in a cabinet that is dry, cool, and dark.

Always recap your oils quickly after use.

5

Treating
Common Ailments
with Aromatherapy

The philosophy of natural medicine holds that the body has
the ability to heal itself. It also holds that biological substances found in nature contain a life force that is an integral part
of the healing process. Together, these two forces stimulate healing while maintaining balance and the homeostasis of bodily systems, without disturbing natural functions.

The life force, the molecular vibration of the plant energy,
cannot be imitated by science. Even with the advances of modern medicine, many plant-derived substances cannot be repro-
duced in a laboratory. Science still relies on plant derivatives for
80 percent of pharmaceutical drugs. Nor can essential oils be
duplicated. For example, essential oil of rose contains 500
chemical compounds, 490 of which are in proportions of less
than 1 percent. All of the constituents of rose oil are known, but
chemists are unable to reproduce the fragrance successfully. It

is the synergy of the whole oil, including the most minuscule components, that creates the power to heal. Each plant from which essential oils are distilled has different medicinal properties, unique unto itself.

Natural remedies often have a beneficial effect on more than one system of the body. This multiaction effect makes plant-based remedies far more useful for common ailments than synthetic pharmaceuticals that have a single action with unpleasant side effects. Aromatherapy works on many levels of the mind and body—one essential oil can affect the psyche and the physical body simultaneously. For example, chamomile oil is indispensable for childhood conditions because of its broad range of action: It is anti-inflammative and a general digestive aid, reduces cramps, relieves gas, and calms the nervous system.

Working in harmony with the body offers many therapeutic benefits. Unlike pharmaceutical drugs, therapy with essential oils is free of unwanted side effects. For instance, the side effects of antibiotic treatment disturb the natural flora that live in the lining of various organs, causing candida (yeast) overgrowth, whereas essential oils reduce candida overgrowth. Harmful microorganisms mutate and become resistant to drugs, causing the rise in infectious diseases once thought to be under control using drug treatment. Aromatherapy, on the other hand, fights infection without creating resistance in disease-causing microorganisms.

Aromatherapy is one of the most powerful forms of botanical medicine because it incorporates the use of highly concentrated substances—large quantities of plant material are used to make just a few drops of oil—and it is effective in treating almost every aspect of health. In this chapter, you will learn many easy and effective treatment methods using a variety of essential oil formulas. As you learn the basic principles of aromatherapy, you can create, blend, and customize therapies to suit particular needs.

DIGESTIVE COMPLAINTS

Aromatherapy improves the function of the digestive system. Volatile oils influence the digestive process by acting on the mucosa and the lining of the intestine. Nervous conditions that cause tension and stomach cramping are helped by the nervine and stress-reducing effects of aromatics that relax muscles. Aromatic nervines tone and soothe the nervous system. The taste and smell of these oils also affect digestion by stimulating saliva and gastric secretions. Disorders such as anorexia nervosa may be helped by using aromatics in scent therapy or topical application. The odor of digestive-supportive essential oils has a stimulating effect on the appetite and increases hunger. Indeed, aromatic herbs and spices, when used in meal preparation, are beneficial in maintaining health and efficient digestion as well as in eliminating wastes and toxins.

47

Antispasmodics

The spasmolytic properties of essential oils are invaluable for treating digestive system disorders. The aromatic constituents have a relaxing effect on the smooth muscle of the intestinal wall, relieving spasms in the gastrointestinal tract. Alpha-bisabolol, a constituent found in peppermint, fennel, cinnamon, chamomile, melissa, caraway, and bitter orange peel (*Citrus aurantium*), is a powerful spasmolytic. Alpha-bisabolol has been found to counteract gastric ulceration, especially ulcers caused by stress and alcohol. The herb chamomile also contains this constituent, in addition to a soothing mucilage that can be extracted by making a tea from the flowers. Drinking the tea can prevent recurrence of gastric ulcer and is beneficial during an acute attack.

Studies have shown that peppermint oil capsules reduce the pain and bloating that accompanies irritable bowel syndrome (IBS), a dysfunction of the large intestine with symptoms that include diarrhea, gas, constipation, nausea, and anxiety. (Enteric-coated capsules should be used in order to bypass the stomach— if peppermint oil is absorbed into the upper digestive tract, acid reflux or heartburn may occur.)

Carminatives

Carminative volatile oils help expel gas and relieve the pain that accompanies flatulence. They work by relaxing the stomach muscle and increasing peristalsis (the involuntary contractions of the digestive muscles), moving food material through the system at a faster rate and reducing distension from gas.

Other conditions such as inflammatory bowel disease and diverticulitis can be helped by the soothing effects of antispasmodic oils as well as carminative aromatic oils. Topical application of both carminative and spasmolytic oils ease the painful cramping that accompanies some digestive conditions. Gently massaging the abdomen in a clockwise direction is helpful after eating or before bed. This is also soothing for children with upset stomachs.

Angelica is helpful in all cases of nervous stomach and tension-related digestive disorders. Angelica is a carminative and has a balancing and calming effect on the nervous system. It is useful in cases of dyspepsia (indigestion), nervous gastritis, and diverticulosis and is a general strengthening tonic for the digestive system.

Peppermint is excellent for relief of nausea. Put a few drops of peppermint oil on a cotton ball and place the ball in a plastic bag. When feeling nauseated, inhale the scent for quick relief.

49

ESSENTIAL OILS FOR THE DIGESTIVE SYSTEM

TYPE	ESSENTIAL OILS
Carminatives	Angelica, aniseed, caraway, cardamom, chamomile, coriander, fennel, ginger, melissa, peppermint, thyme
Spasmolytics	Aniseed, basil, chamomile, caraway, clary sage, cinnamon, fennel, lavender, marjoram, melissa, peppermint, rosemary, thyme

Formulas for Digestive Ailments

Soothing Abdominal Massage Blend

(Helpful for cramps, pain, and general discomfort.)

Chamomile, 8 drops

Angelica, 4 drops

Cardamom, 3 drops

Carrier oil, 1 ounce

Massage onto abdomen as needed.

Tummy Ache Blend for Kids

(Reduce drops of essential oil per ounce of carrier oil according to the age of the child.)

Chamomile, 3 to 5 drops

Citrus aurantium (peel), 1 to 2 drops

Carrier oil, 1 ounce

Pour a small amount of the blend into your palm, allowing the oil to warm before applying. Gently massage in a clockwise direction.

Blend to Stimulate Digestion and Ease Nervous Tension

Tarragon, 7 drops

Clary sage, 4 drops

Caraway, 3 drops

Carrier oil, 1 ounce

Massage onto abdomen as needed.

Anticramp Tea

51

Chamomile, 1 to 3 drops

Honey, 1 teaspoon

Mix and stir into a cup of warm water. Drink before meals.

Tea to Relieve Gas Pains

Peppermint, 1 to 2 drops

Honey, 1 teaspoon

Mix and stir into a cup of warm water. Drink before meals.

Diverticulosis Remedy

Angelica, 1 drop

Chamomile, 1 drop

Pour onto a small piece of bread. Take before meals.

Irritable Bowel Syndrome Remedy

Peppermint oil capsules

(0.2 milliliter of oil per capsule)

Take three times a day between meals. Substitute chamomile if irritation occurs.

Constipation Remedy

(Aromatherapy can reduce the stress and tension that are sometimes the underlying cause of temporary constipation.)

Marjoram, 6 drops

Rosemary, 6 drops

Black pepper or fennel, 3 drops

Carrier oil, 1 ounce

Use this blend for a daily abdominal massage in a clockwise motion.

HEADACHES

Aromatherapy is therapeutic for headaches because of the analgesic and anti-inflammative power of botanical oils, and because the aromas have a relaxing effect and release tension. Local application of peppermint is beneficial for most types of headache, including migraine. Massage a few drops of peppermint and lavender oil into the temples and forehead as necessary (use small quantities, because peppermint stimulates in large doses). When away from home, put a few drops of lavender and peppermint on a handkerchief and sniff as needed.

Sinus Headaches

53

For sinus headaches, do a steam inhalation with 4 drops of eucalyptus oil and 4 drops of either peppermint or niaouli. Add the drops to steaming water, cover your head over the water, and inhale the vapors.

A netti pot is a special container used to wash out the nasal passages (see Resources). To clear the sinuses, do a nasal wash with ¼ teaspoon of sea salt to 1 cup of water.

After the sinuses have been cleared, periodic whiffs of the same oils from an electric aromatherapy diffuser can increase the benefit. Essential oils useful for sinus headaches include rosemary, eucalyptus, lavender, and peppermint.

Migraine

If used at the first sign of an oncoming migraine, aromatherapy may prevent a full-blown attack. Cold compresses (see page 38 for more information) should be applied to the forehead and temples and changed as soon as they warm: Fill a bowl with ice cubes and water and add 3 drops each of lavender and pepper-mint. Some types of migraine involve vascular constriction of blood entering the head. To open the blood vessels, apply warm compresses to the back of the neck with marjoram essential oil. Continue to reapply the compresses while you rest in a dark quiet room until the pain subsides.

Formulas for Headache

Bath

Rosemary, 4 drops

Pine, 2 drops

Eucalyptus, 2 drops

Soak for 20 minutes.

Tension Headache Massage

Rosemary, 4 drops

Lavender, 2 drops

Juniper, 1 drop

Carrier oil, ½ ounce

Apply to the back of the neck and shoulders, and mas-sage until the muscles relax.

INFECTIOUS DISEASE AND IMMUNITY

Botanical medicines have a dual mode of action against infectious diseases: They are toxic to microorganisms, and they stimulate the body's own immunity. Simple aromatherapy treatments fight infection without disturbing the natural flora that protect our internal mucosa and skin from harmful microorganisms. In phytomedicine, this flora, a perfectly balanced colony of healthy protective microorganisms, is an integral part of what is called the terrain. The terrain is the body's first line of defense against pathogens. If the protective terrain of the body deteriorates, it creates an environment that allows unwanted bacteria to thrive.

The use of aromatic medicines, despite their bactericidal properties, does not lead to the development of resistant strains of pathogens as does the use of antibiotics. Overuse and prophylactic use of antibiotics has caused a health crisis in our society. Ever-increasing numbers of bacterial strains have become resistant to antibiotics. In 1941, only 40,000 units per day of penicillin for four days were required to cure pneumococcal pneumonia. Today, a patient could receive 24 million units of penicillin a day, yet die of pneumococcal meningitis. The bacteria *Haemophilus influenzae* causes ear infections, sinusitis, epiglottitis (a disease of part of the larynx), and meningitis. In 1986, thirty-two strains of *H. influenzae* were resistant to ampicillin, a commonly used drug. Today, studies indicate that 50 percent of *H. influenzae* type b strains are resistant to five or more antibiotics, including the most commonly used substitutes for ampicillin, trimethoprim-sulfamethoxazole and chloramphenicol. Bladder infections (cystitis) caused by *E. coli* are extremely common among the elderly; approximately 40 percent of the *E. coli*

55

strains isolated from geriatric patients were found to be resistant to the commonly used drug trimethoprim-sulfamethoxazole.

Holistic medicine supports life and relies strongly on keeping the natural immune mechanisms intact to prevent illness and disease. Essential oils effectively stimulate immunity as they neutralize pathogens. For example, myrrh is toxic against microbes and stimulates the production of leukocytes (white blood cells). Essential oils such as lavender and tea tree disinfect wounds and skin infections without harming surrounding healthy tissue. Essential oils of thyme (*Thymus vulgaris,* thymol and linalol types), savory (*Satureja montana*), and lavender (*Lavandula spica*) elevate the lowered gamma globulin levels associated with chronic bronchitis.

Antibacterial Actions of Essential Oils

Early in this century, essential oils were comparable to the strongest available antiseptic of the day, the synthetic chemical phenol. Thyme was eight times stronger than phenol. Thyme has none of the caustic effects of phenol and when used with prudence is nontoxic. Other antiseptic essential oils more potent than phenol include sweet orange, verbena, rose, clove, eucalyptus, peppermint, orris, and anise.

Paul Balaiche researched the effectiveness of forty-two essential oils against twelve of the most common disease-causing pathogens and published his findings in 1979. As a result of his research, clinical protocols using essential oils as a primary medicine were developed to treat bronchitis, cystitis, childhood illnesses, hepatitis, herpes simplex and zoster (shingles), otitis (ear infections), malaria, rhinitis, sinusitis, skin infections, and tuberculosis. The microorganisms Balaiche tested in vitro were *Escherichia coli, Proteus morganii, Proteus mirabilis* (intestinal infection), *Alcalescens dispar, Corynebacterium xerosis, C. diptheriae* (diphtheria), *Neisseria sub flava* (sinus and ear infection), *Klebsiella* (lung infection), *Streptococcus fecalis* (gram-positive), *Staphylococcus alba* (food poisoning), *Staphylococcus aureus* (which causes pus), *Streptococcus B, Pneumococcus,* and *Candida albicans.*

Aromatics can also rid the air of many of these same bacteria when sprayed in an enclosed room. The most effective essence in inhibiting these microorganisms is oregano, followed (in descending degrees of effectiveness) by thyme, cinnamon, clove, cajeput, rosemary, pine, fennel, lavender, and myrtle.

57

Antiviral Actions of Essential Oils

Many essential oils have antiviral properties. More than a hundred plants in the Lamiaceae family (see chapter 10, "Aromatic Plant Families") have antiviral effects. Cinnamon and eucalyptus are considered just as efficacious against flu as conventional medicine. Studies support the effectiveness of essential oils against chicken pox, mumps, influenza, and polio viruses. The exact mechanism by which essential oils neutralize viruses is not completely known.

Herpes Simplex

For the treatment of herpes, professional aromatherapists suggest bergamot, geranium, *Eucalyptus radiata*, niaouli, tea tree, and rose. Melissa (lemon balm) appears to be unsurpassed in treatment of this condition; it is so effective that the active ingredient has been isolated and is sold in Germany in an antiherpes preparation called Lomaherpan.

To treat herpes, apply the essential oil directly to the lesion. The lesions usually dry within one or two days and heal within three to five days. To prevent an outbreak, apply the following herpes formula to the area as soon as you feel the sensation that signals an eminent outbreak. After using this protocol three or four times, herpes generally does not recur. If irritation occurs, dilute the essential oil in a carrier oil in proportions of 10 percent essential oil to carrier.

Herpes Zoster (Shingles)

58

To treat shingles, a combination of antiviral essential oils, such as ravensara, and a special aromatic fatty oil called calophyllum are used. Calophyllum stimulates immune function, specifically phagocytosis, which cleans waste and toxins from the system. Dramatic improvement should result in seven days from using this formula.

Formulas for Infectious Disease

Herpes (Simplex 1 or 2)

Tea tree, 1 ounce
Calophyllum, 1 ounce

Apply to affected area.

Shingles

Ravensara aromatica, 1 ounce
Calophyllum, 1 ounce

Apply to lesions.

ESSENTIAL OILS FOR INFECTIOUS DISEASE

TYPE	ESSENTIAL OILS
Antibacterial	Oregano, thyme, savory, tea tree, Melaleuca viridiflora (niaouli), Eucalyptus radiata, Ravensara aromatica, lemongrass, Eucalyptus polybractea and E. citriodora, citronella, cinnamon, clove, cajeput, rosemary, pine, fennel, lavender, myrtle
Antifungal	Lavender, geranium, chamomile, tea tree
Antiviral	Melissa, tea tree, juniper, eucalyptus, thyme, palmarosa, lavender, rosemary, clove, laurel, cinnamon bark, anise, rose, Litsea cubeba, lemongrass, geranium, neroli, bergamot, clary sage, dill

MUSCULOSKELETAL INJURIES
AND COMPLAINTS

Many complaints of the muscles and joints are improved by increased circulation, which removes inflammatory wastes and brings fresh nutrient- and oxygen-filled blood to the area. Essential oils penetrate the skin and directly enter the bloodstream; because of this, they easily affect the circulation. Black pepper, rosemary, and ginger are just a few of the aromatic botanicals that stimulate the circulation. Disorders such as arthritis, rheumatism, muscle cramps, back pain, and sports injuries can all benefit from aromatherapeutics.

Analgesics

Analgesic essential oils bring the pain relief essential for the treatment of many conditions. Wintergreen oil contains methyl salicylate, the pain-killing ingredient in aspirin. Menthol, a constituent of peppermint, is known to relieve headache pain. Clove oil is well known for its use in relieving dental pain. Many essential oils are rich in terpenes, chemical constituents that act as a natural analgesic. The relaxant effects of aromatics such as chamomile and ylang-ylang ease the tension that can contribute to pain.

Inflammation

Reducing inflammation plays a major role in treating sports injuries and conditions that affect the joints, such as arthritis. Lavender and arnica are used for joint and muscle pain as well as for general pain relief. Lavender is the oil of choice for inflammation, minor burns, and sunburn. Azulene and chamazulene, found in German chamomile, *Artemisia arborescens,* and yarrow, reduce inflammation and redness, soothing and cooling the injured area. The essential oil of choice for sprained ankles and sports injuries is everlasting (*Helichrysum italicum*). If applied immediately after the injury, this oil dramatically lessens swelling and bruising.

Muscle Cramps

Overexertion can create spasms and tension in the muscles. A sedentary lifestyle can lead to poor circulation in the muscle tissue, causing these tissues to cramp. Essential oils that have a warming effect and increase local blood circulation bring rapid relief. Black pepper, rosemary, and ginger are circulatory stimulants; use these oils in a blend as a topical liniment or in therapeutic baths.

Muscle cramps are often caused by mineral deficiencies due to overexertion or to a poor diet that may lack calcium or potassium, or has an imbalance of salt. Potassium can help normalize the electrical impulses that can cause cramps and twitching muscles. Foods rich in potassium include kelp, parsley, brewer's yeast, beans, sprouts, wheat germ, almonds, sesame seeds, salmon, halibut, avocados, peanuts, rye, liver, lentils, buckwheat, potatoes, and bananas. To avoid potassium depletion during exercise and other periods of heavy perspiration, try drinking this "mineral cocktail."

61

Mineral Cocktail

Pure water, 16 ounces

Juice of 2 lemons

Raw honey, 1 tablespoon

Natural sea salt, ¼–½ teaspoon

ESSENTIAL OILS FOR THE MUSCULOSKELETAL SYSTEM

TYPE	ESSENTIAL OILS
Analgesic	Anise, coriander, clove, cinnamon, eucalyptus, geranium, ginger, lavender, black pepper, juniper, niaouli, nutmeg, marjoram, rosemary, sage, peppermint, pine, wintergreen

Formulas for the Musculoskeletal System

Bath to Reduce Heat and Inflammation

Lavender, 4 drops

Eucalyptus, 2 drops

Apple cider vinegar, 2 cups

Soak the affected area for 20 minutes.

Warm-Up Oil

> Black pepper, 7 drops
>
> Rosemary, 6 drops
>
> Juniper, 5 drops
>
> Arnica oil, 1 ounce

Massage into muscles before exercise to stimulate circulation.

Analgesic Blend

(Indicated for arthritis, back pain, and general pain.)

> Eucalyptus, 2 drops
>
> Lavender, 10 drops
>
> Wintergreen, 6 drops
>
> Carrier oil, 1 ounce

Massage into affected area to relieve pain.

Ginger Bath for Stiff and Sore Muscles

Make a tea of 1½ cups grated ginger. Pour the strained liquid into bath. Add 6 drops of rosemary essential oil. Soak for 20 minutes.

Hot Bath with Epsom Salts for Stiff and Sore Muscles

Rosemary, 6 drops

Juniper, 5 drops

Lavender, 3 drops

Epsom salts, 2 cups

Add all the ingredients to a hot bath. Soak for 25 minutes.

Formula to Prevent Swelling and Bruises

Everlasting, 10 drops

German chamomile, 5 drops

Carrier oil, 1 ounce

Apply immediately to injury.

NERVOUS CONDITIONS

Aromatherapy can be incorporated into one's life to increase health and wellness on many levels. Aromatics have a multitude of effects on the mind and emotions because of their direct contact with the limbic system (discussed in chapter 2, "How Aromatherapy Works"). Skin penetration also allows for a second avenue of effect via the nervous system. Topical application and massage stimulate touch receptors, which activate the release of various neurotransmitters and hormones, triggering immediate bodily reactions. The effects of aromatic massage on the mind and on bodily functions such as heart rate, breathing, and muscle tension can create a powerful change in both emotions and physiology.

The sympathetic nervous system prepares us for possible danger with the fight-or-flight response. During a crisis, adrenaline is released, and blood flow to the muscles and limbs needed to fight and to run is increased. Heart rate and breathing become rapid. Digestion slows, and the skin becomes pale as blood flow is routed into the muscles. Once the crisis is over, the parasympathetic nervous system relaxes muscles and slows heart rate and breathing. The stress of modern life often triggers the fight-or-flight response, leaving us without any physical outlet for this adrenalized state. To reduce the stress and anxiety that result from this chronic overstimulation, we can tone and calm the sympathetic and central nervous systems using restorative and relaxant essential oils.

65

Relaxants and Sedatives

Oils in the relaxant category reduce states of nervous excitement and treat sleep problems. EEG tests of the brain's rhythm patterns found that neroli, jasmine, and rose induced delta rhythms, with some inducing a combination of delta and theta rhythms. Delta and theta rhythms are associated with reducing mental chatter and allowing for more intuitive thought processes.

Melissa is an aromatic botanical with a long reputation for having calming properties. Avicenna, the ancient physician, said the herb "makes the heart merry." Recent research has found that melissa affects the limbic system and is sedative. Melissa is used for nervous heart (a heart prone to palpitations and tachycardia, an abnormally fast heartbeat), depression, restlessness, excitement, headache, and insomnia.

Tonics and Restoratives

The tonics are used to support and strengthen the nervous system. Nervous debility is often an underlying factor in depression. Tonics are useful in these cases, as well as in cases of convalescence from illness, extreme stress, and shock.

Neroli, a restorative oil that reduces tension and anxiety, has both tonic and relaxant properties, inducing calm and sleep. Chamomile calms and relieves tension. It is beneficial for insomnia, anger, depression, and oversensitivity.

Stimulants

Stimulant essential oils are used for conditions of mental fatigue, poor memory, and difficulty concentrating. Stimulants are useful when you're feeling tired or sluggish and need to boost your mental activity. EEG tests used to evaluate stimulant essential oils such as black pepper, cardamom, and rosemary indicated that they induced beta brain rhythms. Beta rhythms correlate with aroused attention and alertness.

Some oils, such as rosemary, are both tonic and stimulant to the nervous system. Rosemary is a brain stimulant; it produces a feeling of mental clarity and aids in mental capacity. Rosemary has been used to treat the loss or reduction of sensory functions, such as temporary paralysis (in cases where nerve tissue is not irreversibly damaged), speech impairment, and loss of smell. Diffuse 3 to 6 drops in an aroma lamp in your workplace, or drink a cup of rosemary tea.

Treatment of Depression and Anxiety

Aromatherapy is a useful tool in conjunction with other therapies to help produce more positive feelings. To support emotional healing, touch—whether in the form of a massage from a professional aromatherapist or self-massage, such as foot massage—can greatly enhance recovery.

For depression, choose stimulant and tonic essential oils, such as jasmine and angelica, to be used at least three times a week in baths and foot massages. Melissa (lemon balm) herbal tea is antidepressant and may be incorporated into your regime. Brew 1 teaspoon of herb per cup of boiling water; drink 1 to 3 cups a day.

To treat anxiety, choose sedative and tonic oils such as marjoram and lavender, and use them three times a week or more for baths and foot massages. Chamomile and oatstraw teas are beneficial for anxiety. Brew 1 teaspoon of herb per cup of boiling water; the recommended dosage is 1 to 3 cups a day.

To quickly alter your mood, carry a handkerchief to which you have applied a few drops of the appropriate essential oil and inhale as necessary.

ESSENTIAL OILS FOR THE NERVOUS SYSTEM

TYPE	ESSENTIAL OILS
Relaxants and sedatives	Chamomile, bergamot, *Citrus aurantium,* petitgrain, geranium, neroli, lavender, mandarin, marjoram, melissa, sandalwood, angelica, valerian
Tonics and restoratives	Angelica, basil, rose, cypress, lavender, marjoram, neroli, rosemary, bitter orange, hyssop, spikenard, sage, patchouli
Stimulants	Basil, lemon, coriander, cardamom, cinnamon, jasmine, peppermint, eucalyptus, juniper, rosemary, tea tree, fennel, geranium, thyme, cloves, pine, verbena, ylang-ylang
To prevent or relieve panic attacks	Jasmine, melissa, neroli, ylang-ylang, frankincense, rose, lemon, verbena

68

Formulas for Depression and Anxiety

Antidepressant Aroma Lamp or Diffuser Treatment

Basil, 5 drops

Antidepressant Stimulating Massage

Rosemary, 7 drops

Carrier oil, 1 ounce

Massage along spine.

Antidepressant Foot Massage Blend

Angelica, 5 drops

Cardamom, 6 drops

Basil, 2 drops

Carrier oil, 1 ounce

69

Antidepressant Bath

Jasmine, 2 drops

Rose, 2 drops

Melissa, 1 drop

Add to bath water.

Antianxiety Massage Blend

Spikenard, 4 drops

Chamomile, 7 drops

Sandalwood, 3 drops

Carrier oil, 1 ounce

Massage the feet before bed. In the morning, use the blend to anoint the pulse points on the wrists, the back of the neck, and the solar plexus.

70

Antianxiety Bath

Chamomile, 3 drops

Lavender, 3 drops

Mandarin, 1 drop

Add to bath water.

Antianxiety Aroma Lamp or Diffuser Treatment

Neroli, 3 drops

Chamomile, 2 drops

Anti-Insomnia Treatment

Marjoram, 1 drop

Place on your pillow before bed.

Anti-Insomnia Bath

Marjoram, 4 drops
Chamomile, 2 drops

Add to bath water.

Treatment to Relieve Nervous Tension or Insomnia

Sesame oil, ½ cup
Marjoram or sandalwood, 5 drops

Warm the sesame oil, then add the essential oils. To calm nerves, massage the warm blend onto your skin after a bath. (Sesame oil is part of the ayurvedic pharmacy used to pacify the *vata* constitution, which, when out of balance, is prone to nervousness and insomnia.)

RESPIRATORY COMPLAINTS

Essential oils are ideal substances for treating respiratory system conditions. The volatility of aromatics allows for their easy inhalation into the nasal passages and lungs as the molecules become airborne. This brings the essential oils into direct contact with the infected area for localized treatment.

Essential oils have multiple effects against respiratory ailments because of their expectorant, mucolytic, and anti-infectious properties. Expectorants help clear the lungs by expelling mucus. The inhalation of even very small doses of essential oils increases bronchial secretions and produces an expectorant effect. Even essential oils that enter the body by pathways other than the lungs are excreted through exhalation. Essential oils such as pine, thyme, fennel, and anise contain the oxide constituent 1,8 cineole, which has expectorant properties.

Mucolytics, primarily of the ketone group (see page 21), are an integral part of the treatment protocol. Mucolytics thin mucus secretions so congestion can be expelled.

Treatment for respiratory conditions combines essential oils to thin mucus, with expectorants to clear congestion, and antibacterial, antimicrobial aromatics. These three aspects of this botanical protocol make for a highly effective treatment.

Expectorant and Mucolytic Oils

Inula graveolens, which contains sesquiterpene lactones, is a powerful mucolytic (a substance that breaks down mucus). It is highly recommended for bronchitis and conditions of the sinus and throat. *Inula* is also antispasmodic, so in cases of chest spasm and tension from excessive coughing, *Inula* has a double benefit.

Anise is an expectorant that is also antiseptic to the mucous membranes. Its spasmolytic properties help relax the muscles of the lung. Traditionally, anise was used as an herbal infusion for colic in babies. High doses can be neurotoxic, however, and anise should not be used by young children or pregnant women. Older children can use anise in the form of a weak herbal tea or as part of a formula to break up congestion. Anise is indicated for whooping cough, bronchitis, and dry irritated cough. It works well in formulas or alone in low doses. Anise essential oil is for topical use only; the herb itself is equally beneficial as a tea.

Rosemary verbenone is a chemotype of rosemary—that is, a chemical variety of *Rosemary officinalis*. It is used in the early stages of a respiratory infection for its mucolytic effect. It is especially beneficial for colds and bronchitis. Rosemary verbenone should not be used by pregnant women or by children younger than ten.

Bactericidal and Fungicidal Oils

After the mucolytic essential oils are used to clear congestion, we introduce bactericidal and fungicidal plant oils to fight the infection. Essential oils in this category include eucalyptus, *Ravensara aromatica*, tea tree, thyme, and lavender. These botanicals traditionally were used to combat a wide variety of infections, and modern research continues to support their use. The *Thymus vulgaris* chemotype thymol has been found to be highly effective against bacteria and microbes such as *Candida albicans*, *Escherichia coli*,

Klebsiella, and *Diplococcus pneumoniae.* Lavender and tea tree have been found very effective against *Candida albicans, Diplococcus pneumoniae,* and *Escherichia coli.*

The antiseptic properties of essential oils make them a viable alternative to antibiotic use. Although antibiotics are necessary in serious or life-threatening situations, antiseptic aromatics used for common respiratory complaints offer an avenue of treatment that does not create resistant strains of microorganisms, which are becoming more and more prevalent as diseases thought to be under control by modern medicine are once again taking lives.

74

Prevention

Essential oils can be used as a prophylactic to disinfect the environment. During cold and flu season, use an aromatherapy diffuser to vaporize antiseptic essential oils. (This method can be especially effective in waiting rooms and office environments.) People often catch respiratory infections on airplanes. To help protect your throat and nasal passages against germs while traveling, place a few drops of tea tree oil on a cotton handkerchief, store it in a plastic bag, and periodically inhale the scent. When colds are spreading at your child's school, massage a blend of child-safe essential oils on the child's chest and neck lymph nodes (sides of the neck from the ears to the collarbone). A good antiseptic blend for children is 5 drops of lavender mixed with 1 ounce of carrier.

Method of Use

Several methods may be used to inhale the essences. An electric diffuser can be kept in the bedroom on a low setting to disperse the essential oil throughout the night. For steam inhalation, add a few drops of essential oil to simmering water, place a towel over your head, and inhale the vapors. Be sure not to get too close to the water to avoid burns. For topical application of a blended mixture over the chest, throat, or sinus area, massage the oil well into your skin, and cover your neck with a scarf and your chest with a flannel to allow the oils to penetrate more deeply. A drop of essence on a pillowcase is helpful to relieve minor congestion.

75

℘

ESSENTIAL OILS FOR THE RESPIRATORY SYSTEM

TYPE	ESSENTIAL OILS
Expectorant	Pine, thyme, eucalyptus, fennel, anise
Anti-infectious	Tea tree, eucalyptus, thyme, *Ravensara aromatica,* hyssop, niaouli, lavender, oregano

---

Formulas for Respiratory Ailments

Respiratory Infection Blend

Tea tree, 8 drops

Lavender, 5 drops

Ravensara, 3 drops

Niaouli, 1 drop

Carrier oil, 1 ounce

Massage over infected area (chest, throat, or sinus) 3 times a day.

Steam Blend to Loosen Mucus Congestion

Eucalyptus, 6 drops

Tea tree, 2 drops

Add to simmering water. Inhale steam for 15 to 20 minutes. Add more essential oils as needed.

Sore Throat Gargle

Tea tree, 3 drops

Sea salt, ⅛ teaspoon

Warm water, 1 cup

Gargle as needed.

Mucolytic/Expectorant Formula

Inula graveolens, 4 drops

Eucalyptus, 8 drops

Thyme, 4 drops

Carrier oil, 1 ounce

Massage over infected area (chest, throat, or sinus) 3 times a day.

SEXUALLY TRANSMITTED DISEASES

Chlamydia

Chlamydia is the most common sexually transmitted disease in the United States. Often people infected with the disease do not have symptoms, but are still able to infect others. The consequences of untreated chlamydia are serious; this infection can cause infertility in women. Chlamydia infections may recur, even with antibiotic treatment. For this reason, it's a good idea to use vaginal suppositories made with thuja oil, a potent antibacterial and antiviral that has been found effective against this infection, in addition to antibiotic therapy. Betadine douche, sold at pharmacies, is also effective against chlamydia infection. Alternate the douche with vaginal suppositories if sensitivity or irritation occurs.

Caution: Treatment with suppositories should be under the supervision of a health-care professional. Alternative treatment is not a substitute for medical care; use only in addition to

77

medically prescribed antibiotic therapy. Essential oils can damage latex condoms, so sexual abstinence is recommended during treatment. Thuja oil is for short-term use only, and the recommended dose should not be exceeded. Thuja oil is toxic if ingested; keep it away from children (see pages 126–129 on safety and toxicity).

Vaginal Suppository for Chlamydia

Suppository base, 1 ounce
(such as cocoa butter or gelatin)

Suppository molds
(available from your pharmacist)

Thuja, 2½ milliliters

Tea tree, 1½ milliliters

Melt suppository base in a sterile saucepan until almost liquid. Stir in essential oils and mix thoroughly. Pour into molds. Refrigerate. Use one per night for at least 20 days.

Boosting immunity and taking sufficient nutrients such as vitamin E and zinc is an important part of chlamydia therapy. Daily recommended supplements are vitamin E (400 IU), vitamin A (10,000 IU), vitamin C (1,000 milligrams four times a day), and zinc gluconate (30 milligrams).

Herbal therapy may be incorporated into the treatment protocol: barberry tincture (*Berberis*), 10 to 60 drops three times a day; or goldenseal tincture (*Hydrastis*), 6 to 12 milliliters three times a day. To stimulate immunity, use 30 to 100 drops of an echinacea tincture five times a day, and 30 to 60 drops of *Astragalus* tincture four times a day.

Human Papilloma Virus
(Venereal Warts)

Possibly between 40 and 80 percent of the American population is infected with a sexually transmitted disease called human papilloma virus (HPV). The majority of individuals who are infected with HPV have no symptoms. If symptoms are visible, they will be small warts that resemble cauliflower on the genitals. HPV may have serious consequences for women. It is associated with changes in the cells of the cervix, which can progress to abnormalities such as dysplasia and cervical cancer.

The antiviral properties of thuja essential oil are effective in treating HPV. For treatment of the cervical warts, use the vaginal suppositories and treatment protocol listed under chlamydia on pages 77 to 78. For warts on the external genitals or anus, carefully apply undiluted thuja oil *to the wart only*, using a cotton swab. Be careful not to get thuja oil on the surrounding skin or mucous membranes; irritation and burning may occur. Repeat the application once a day until the condition has cleared.

Folic acid is an essential nutrient for the health of the female reproductive organs. After the onset of HPV, take a 10-milligram folic acid supplement for three months, then a 2.5-milligram folic acid supplement for the next year.

HPV is a serious medical condition; its treatment should be under the supervision of a medical professional.

SKIN DISORDERS

The skin is the largest organ of the body and serves many functions. It guards our internal organs from harm. It is part of the immune system, acting as the first line of defense against infection. Beneficial microorganisms that inhabit the skin's surface protect it from invading microorganisms, as does its protective coating of lactic acid and sodium mixed with sebaceous secretions, which is in itself antibacterial. This protective coating also acts as a humectant, holding in moisture. Our skin is also an organ of elimination, ridding the body of one-fourth of its toxic waste.

Because of these factors, the overall health of the body is often reflected in the condition of the skin. Substances taken internally that affect blood composition are detected in the hair and skin. Aspirin can be detected by hair analysis only nine hours after ingestion. Toxins not eliminated in the liver that have built up in the blood circulation often appear as surface skin disorders or an unpleasant body odor. Conditions such as eczema, psoriasis, and acne reflect imbalance in the body as whole.

The skin also absorbs nutrients, such as vitamin D from sunshine. The absorption of vitamin D, a fat-soluble vitamin, is facilitated by a proper lipid balance in the skin. This is why it's important not to strip the skin of its protective layer of oil. Application of high-quality fatty oils, such as hazelnut, helps maintain the oil balance of the skin. Hazelnut oil contains lipid-soluble, absorbable vitamins such as E, A, and D.

When fatty oils are blended with essential oils, each can penetrate the skin more deeply. The fatty oil mixes with sebaceous secretions, and the essential oil has a solvent effect on the sebum, allowing for rapid penetration. Essential oils encourage oxygenation in the cellular tissues. Aromatic oils increase circulation and the overall efficiency of the skin's functions.

Eczema

Eczema is characterized by dry, itching, inflamed patches of skin. Also called atopic dermatitis, it typically appears on the face, scalp, and limbs. Allergies appear to play a role in eczema. Common food allergens such as wheat gluten and dairy may contribute to the problem. Dairy products from cows are often primary allergens. Children who have been breast-fed have less incidence of hayfever and asthma, conditions that appear to be related to eczema.

Evening primrose oil capsules are beneficial in reducing the inflammatory response in this condition. Herbs traditionally used to treat disorders of the skin focus on purification of the blood and liver; primary examples are red clover, burdock, and Oregon grape. Take 2 to 3 cups of red clover tea a day. Use burdock and Oregon grape in tincture form. Comfrey is well known for its ability to heal skin conditions. For weeping eczema, make a tea of comfrey and apply the liquid as a compress. To make a comfrey poultice, pour just enough boiling water over the herb to moisten it to a slippery consistency. When it has cooled, apply it to the affected area. Cover with gauze and tape down with first-aid tape.

Essential oils also hasten healing of this condition. Aromatics such as German chamomile reduce inflammation, regenerate skin tissue, and soothe discomfort and itching.

Psoriasis

Psoriasis is characterized by sharply defined red patches with silvery scales. It is caused by a buildup of skin cells that have replicated faster than they can be shed. Studies have shown that supplementation with fish oil capsules can greatly improve this condition. Essential fatty acids, such as those found in flaxseed oil and cold-water fish like mackerel and salmon, can offer similar benefits.

Topical application of chamomile oil benefits many skin conditions characterized by dry, flaky skin. Chamomile has significant anti-inflammatory properties and is antiallergic. Herbal preparations containing extracts of the herb licorice root have also been successful in treating psoriasis. During a psoriasis breakout, drink 2 to 3 cups a day of a licorice root decoction and use some of the decoction as a compress. To make a licorice root decoction, simmer 1 teaspoon of root per cup of water for twenty minutes. *Caution*: Persons with high blood pressure should not use licorice.

Boils and Abscesses

Boils and abscesses are active infections of the skin. The nutrients vitamin C (500 milligrams taken four to six times a day) and zinc (50 milligrams taken once a day) increase immunity and help fight infection. To support the immune system, *Echinacea purpurea* tincture taken internally (30 to 100 drops three to five times a day) or as a tea (3 to 4 cups a day) is very beneficial. Follow this regime for two weeks.

To draw the infection to the skin's surface, make a poultice of fenugreek seed (simply boil the fenugreek in water), then mix with 3 drops of thyme oil. Apply the warm mass to the boil and cover with a cloth to keep it warm. In addition, you can apply goldenseal powder moistened with water and mixed with 4 drops of tea tree oil. Apply the paste to the boil three or four times a day. Once the boil has drained, apply 2 to 3 drops of tea tree oil four or five times a day until it is healed. Also, St. John's wort tincture may be applied daily.

Rashes and Irritations

Rashes and irritations are quickly soothed by anti-inflammative essential oils. Lavender oil is a necessity in the first-aid chest for burns, bug bites, and most common skin complaints. For insect bites, apply a drop straight out of the bottle. For minor burns, apply the same way. For skin irritations, mix 7 to 15 drops in 1 ounce of hazelnut oil and apply three times a day. For stubborn rashes, use the anti-inflammatory blends on page 86.

Acne

Many factors cause acne; however, hormonal interactions are a particularly strong contributor. The increase of testosterone at the onset of puberty increases sebaceous secretions, causing comedones (blackheads). When the pores become blocked, they are prone to the bacterial growth that causes acne.

Young women often suffer from acne premenstrually. A healthy, whole-foods diet is recommended, including alkaline foods such as dark, leafy greens, brown rice, millet, and buckwheat. Eat plenty of raw vegetables, which will provide proper nutrients and fiber. Fast food, refined sugar, and carbonated drinks can aggravate acne and should be avoided. Vitamin A and zinc supplements help build skin immunity.

Constipation sometimes exacerbates acne. To help elimination, add fiber such as ½ cup oat bran cereal for breakfast, or before bed make a tea from 1 teaspoon psyllium seeds and 1 cup warm water.

A special massage technique called manual lymph drainage is very helpful in clearing acne. It involves localized treatment of the head and neck by a trained professional and is used to detoxify the lymphatic system and stimulate healing of acne lesions.

A combination approach to healing acne is most effective. Diet and herbs stimulate healing internally, and essential oils fight the infection, regenerate skin tissue, and aid in skin detoxification. Herbal preparations beneficial for acne include Oregon grape (*Mahonia*) tincture (10 to 60 drops three times a day) for face and neck acne; black walnut (*Juglans*) tincture (30 to 90 drops three times a day) for acne with constipation; burdock root (*Arctium*) tincture (30 to 90 drops three times a day) for chronic acne; and Siberian ginseng (*Eleutherococcus*) and *Panax ginseng* (20 to 60 drops of a tincture or 2 to 3 ounces of an infusion, both three times a day) for hormonal acne.

Recent studies have shown that tea tree oil is just as effective in treating acne as benzoyl peroxide, a commonly used acne preparation. Benzoyl peroxide is irritating to the skin, and animal studies suggest that it is a possible carcinogen. In contrast, tea tree oil is completely safe, nonirritating, and without side effects. For the occasional pimple, apply 1 drop of tea tree oil directly to acne spots. For widespread acne, make a 15 percent dilution by mixing 15 milliliters of tea tree oil with 100 milliliters of a carrier such as a nongreasy, unscented white lotion (often sold in bulk at health-food stores). Apply to lesions three or four times a day.

Weeping Eczema Compress

Birch, 4 drops
Bowl of cool water

Apply compress to affected area. Reapply every 15 minutes.

85

Weeping Eczema Blend

Thyme, 10 drops
Cajeput, 10 drops
Calophyllum, ½ ounce
Rosehip seed oil, 1 ounce

Apply to lesions 4 times a day.

Dry Eczema Treatment

German chamomile, 15 drops

Calendula, ½ ounce

Aloe vera gel, 1 ounce

Mix thoroughly. Shake before use. Apply to lesions 4 times a day. (If the aloe gel is from a fresh plant, keep it refrigerated.)

Anti-Inflammative Lotion for Eczema

German chamomile, 25 drops

St. John's wort, 20 milliliters

Unscented white lotion, 2 ounces

Mix thoroughly. Shake before use. Apply to lesions 4 times a day.

Anti-Inflammatory Blend for Psoriasis

German chamomile, 9 drops

Helichrysum italicum, 4 drops

Rosemary verbenone, 2 drops

Hazelnut oil, 1 ounce

Rosehip seed oil, 1 teaspoon

Apply to area 2 or 3 times a day.

Cooling Bath for Overexposure to the Sun or the Elements, or to Calm Irritation from Insect Bites

Lavender, 4 drops

Tea tree, 1 drop

Eucalyptus, 1 drop

Apple cider vinegar, 1 cup

Add to bath water.

Facial Clearing Steam for Acne

Lemon, 2 drops

Lavender, 3 drops

Ylang-ylang, 2 drops

Add to 1 quart of steaming water.

Oatmeal Scrub for Acne

Tea tree, 2 drops

Lavender, 1 drop

Uncooked oatmeal, 1 teaspoon

Mix with oatmeal until moistened. Gently massage into skin and rinse with cool water.

Acne Scar Formula

Rosemary verbenone, 10 drops

Helichrysum italicum, 5 drops

Grapeseed oil, 1 ounce

Vitamin E, 4 capsules

Apply nightly.

Premenstrual Acne (Acne Related to Hormonal Imbalance) Formula

Clary sage, 7 drops

Geranium, 4 drops

Palmarosa, 1 drop

Grapeseed oil, 1 ounce

Apply to skin morning and night.

Acne Blend

Tea tree, 15 drops

Lavender, 10 drops

Bergamot or thyme, 2 drops

Grapeseed oil, 1½ ounce

Apply to blemished area.

6

Treating
Women's Ailments
with Aromatherapy

Botanicals have been used for centuries to treat female complaints. Plant medicine has been used to tonify the system in preparation for childbirth and to regulate menstrual disorders. Emotional imbalances in women (once called hysteria) were treated with nervines.

Modern medicine recognizes that hormonal imbalances can lead to mood swings and other emotional imbalances, which are associated with premenstrual syndrome (PMS) and menopause. Stress increases the adrenal hormone cortisol, which in turn causes other imbalances in the endocrine system, such as lowered progesterone. Aromatherapy plays a role in alleviating all these conditions particular to women, with the added benefit of wonderfully reducing stress and tension.

HORMONAL EFFECTS

Clary sage has long been used as a menstrual regulator. Its chemical constituent sclereol is estrogenlike and is useful for both PMS and amenorrhea. Fennel also has an estrogenic effect and traditionally was used to promote the flow of breast milk and to treat dysmenorrhea. The aromatic components viridiflorol and trans-anethole (found in anise) have chemical structures similar to estrogen and folliculin. Compounds in pine (*Pinus sylvestris*) are similar to cortisone. Geranium, basil, sage, rosemary, savory, and pine all stimulate the adrenal cortex. Cypress may be a homologue (i.e., a substitute) to ovarian hormone.

TONICS

Aromatic tonics strengthen and tonify the reproductive system and often balance the nervous system. Tonics may be incorporated into almost any formula to enhance its effect. Rose, a nerve tonic, has long been associated with the feminine and has an affinity for both male and female reproductive organs. Rose cleanses and strengthens the uterus. It is indicated for irregular menstruation, cramps, vaginitis, and postpartum depression. It also has a reputation as a liver cleanser.

Geranium, a general tonic, is indicated for yeast infections (*Candida albicans*) and painful breasts. It is helpful for postpartum bleeding because of its hemostatic (it stops bleeding) properties.

CRAMPS AND DYSMENORRHEA
(Painful Periods)

All of the antispasmodic essences relax tension in the uterine muscle and help relieve pain and cramping. These oils include chamomile, caraway, fennel, angelica, cardamom, and clary sage. Clary sage is of primary importance in treating cramps and dysmenorrhea because of its calming effect on the nervous system, its hormone-balancing effect, and its ability to reduce spasms. A warm herb tea made with equal parts of angelica, chamomile, and fennel will also relieve cramps. Use 1 teaspoon of the herbs in 1 cup of boiling water.

91

CANDIDA ALBICANS
(Vaginal Yeast Infection)

Candida is a naturally occurring bacteria that lives in the vagina. When the flora (i.e., healthy bacteria and other microorganisms) of the vagina are in balance, *Candida* stays in check. If the acid pH is disturbed, yeast overgrowth can occur. Antifungal essential oils kill *Candida* without disturbing the healthy flora of the vagina. Tea tree and geranium are both antifungal agents. Tea tree suppositories have powerful antiyeast activity and are an easy way to treat the infection. The dosage is 200 milligrams in one suppository per day on alternate days for seven to ten days. Tea tree suppositories are sold at some health-food stores, or an aromatherapist or herbalist can make them for you.

An alternative treatment is to soak a natural cotton tampon with a mixture of 6 drops of tea tree, 2 drops of geranium, and 1 tablespoon of calendula oil. Insert into the vagina and remember to remove it at night. After removing the tampon before bed, insert 2 capsules of acidophilus into the vagina to replenish the healthy bacteria.

A third method is to mix 6 drops of tea tree and 2 drops of marjoram with 1 ounce of natural cultured yogurt. Fill a plastic syringe with the mixture and inject into the vagina. Follow this regime daily until the condition clears.

VAGINITIS

(*Trichomonas*)

A study of ninety-six patients with vaginitis caused by *Trichomonas vaginalis* and *Candida albicans* found that tea tree oil, administered by a combination of douche and tampon applications, was effective in resolving the infection. The oil has antibacterial, antifungal, and antiprotozoal properties.

Note: Trichomonas infection is a medical condition. Its treatment should be supervised by a health professional.

AMENORRHEA

Amenorrhea is the absence of menstruation, excluding prepuberty, pregnancy, and menopause. Amenorrhea can be caused by a variety of factors. For instance, low body fat may disrupt menstruation; hormones are manufactured from cholesterol, so appropriate dietary fat intake is necessary to maintain many bodily functions.

Another cause may be a lack of ovulation, which may be stimulated by a combination of herbal medicine and aromatherapy with hormonal influences. *Vitex agnus-castus* (chaste berry) stimulates luteinizing hormone (LH), which in turn signals the ovaries to release a mature egg into the fallopian tube in readiness for fertilization. The usual dose is 1 squirt of a *Vitex* tincture first thing in the morning. Keep in mind that this treatment may take six weeks to five months to take effect. The diet should also contain at least 50 milligrams of vitamin B_6, which affects LH and progesterone levels in a similar way.

Emmenagogues are substances that bring on menstruation. Essential oils in this category are an important part of an amenorrhea formula. They include chamomile, yarrow, basil, fennel, lavender, cinnamon, nutmeg, oregano, marjoram, caraway, hyssop, peppermint, rosemary, sage, and thyme.

IRREGULAR
MENSTRUAL CYCLES

Irregular cycles can be caused by the same factors as amenorrhea and are treated with the same protocols. Although ovulation may occur in some cycles, the quality of the corpus luteum—a temporary organ formed after ovulation that produces progesterone and maintains the lining of the uterus until either menses or pregnancy occurs—may produce insufficient progesterone for menstruation to occur regularly. Follow the guidelines on page 94 for *Vitex,* B_6, and aromatherapy formulas.

PREMENSTRUAL SYNDROME
(PMS)

It is believed that high estrogen levels paired with low progesterone levels are responsible for PMS symptoms. PMS includes
a variety of symptoms that differ from woman to woman and
month to month. These include irritability, mood swings, anxiety, nervousness, breast tenderness, and fluid retention. *Vitex*
helps increase progesterone levels. The dosage is 1 dropperful of
Vitex tincture first thing in the morning. Evening primrose oil
reduces breast tenderness and cramps by increasing prostaglan-
din 1 (PG1) levels. PG1 reduces the inflammatory response and
is responsible for many beneficial bodily functions. The dosage
for evening primrose oil is 3 grams two times a day with meals.
Vitamin B_6, which influences hormone levels, and magnesium
are also helpful.

Aromatherapy treatment for PMS focuses on reducing
fluid retention, relieving tension, and stabilizing moods and
emotions. Juniper oil, one of the most efficient diuretics in aromatherapy, can alleviate the first complaint. After work, take a
few moments to unwind and have a juniper foot bath: Add 6 to
8 drops to warm water and soak for twenty minutes. Neroli tar-
gets the nervous system, acting as an antidepressant, sedative, and
relaxant. Clary sage balances hormones and helps relieve anxiety
and irritability. Ylang-ylang is relaxing and calms the heart palpitations that sometimes accompany PMS.

CYSTITIS

Cystitis is an infection of the urinary tract common to many women. At the first sign of infection, drink plenty of unsweetened, 100 percent cranberry juice. Cranberries make the lining of the urethra slippery, preventing the adherence of bacteria.

Yarrow has an affinity for the urinary system and may be used to ease discomfort. Mix 7 drops of yarrow with 1 ounce of castor oil, then massage onto the lower abdomen. Warm applications may ease the pain, depending on the stage of inflammation. Apply a compress (see page 38) of the yarrow mixture, then cover with plastic and a dry towel.

Sandalwood is antiseptic for the urinary tract and can be used in conjunction with herbal remedies to relieve cystitis. To blend a disinfectant formula, use ½ ounce of uva-ursi tincture, ¼ ounce of thyme tincture, ¼ ounce of echinacea tincture, and 5 drops of sandalwood. Take ¼ teaspoon in 1 cup of warm water every two to three hours when symptoms first appear, then twice a day for several days.

Environmental note: Both *Echinacea augustifolia* and sandalwood reserves are diminishing. As a substitute for *E. augustifolia*, use *Echinacea purpurea*, a cultivated plant that is equally effective medicinally and not endangered. Use sandalwood with prudence. The trees are being harvested at a rapid rate, and their supply cannot be readily replenished because the sandalwood tree takes 100 years to fully mature.

95

MENOPAUSE

To alleviate the discomforts of menopause, a variety of aromas are beneficial. For hot flashes, cool compresses bring immediate relief. Add 4 to 6 drops of lavender oil to a bowl of cold water, dip in a cloth, wring out the excess water, and sponge off the forehead, the back of the neck, and the wrists. Another quick remedy that can be used when away from home is a drop of lavender oil dabbed on your inner wrist or temples. Keep a bottle of lavender in your purse and use as needed.

Neroli blossom is a highly beneficial essence for the nervous system because of its antidepressant properties. Use 3 or 4 drops of neroli essential oil in an aroma lamp or a diffuser to uplift moods. Melissa (lemon balm) is also indicated for depression and nervous tension. To make an iced tea of the herb, use 1 teaspoon per cup of boiling water, then add the juice of 1 lemon. Refrigerate when cool. Drink 1 cup as needed.

ESSENTIAL OILS FOR THE FEMALE REPRODUCTIVE SYSTEM

TYPE	ESSENTIAL OILS
Primary oils	Rose, neroli, ylang-ylang, geranium, fennel, yarrow, chamomile, angelica, spikenard, melissa
Aphrodisiacs	Black pepper, cardamom, clary sage, neroli, jasmine, rose, sandalwood, patchouli, ylang-ylang
Anaphrodisiac (to reduce sexual desire)	Marjoram

Formulas for Women's Ailments

Cramps

Clary sage, 8 drops

Chamomile, 5 drops

Angelica (or cardamom), 2 to 3 drops

Carrier oil, 1 ounce

Massage onto the abdomen and lower back as needed. After the application of oils, you may place a towel and hot water bottle over the affected area.

Dysmenorrhea (Painful Periods)

Chamomile, 3 drops

Yarrow, 3 drops

Add to bath after tub is full. Soak for 20 minutes. For a compress treatment, add the same essential oils to a bowl of warm water, dip a flannel in the water, wring out, and apply to the affected area.

PMS No More Anxiety
Aroma Lamp or Diffuser Treatment

Clary sage, 6 drops

Amenorrhea and Irregular Cycles, Formula 1

Basil, 4 drops

Fennel, 8 drops

Rose or geranium, 3 drops

Carrier oil, 1 ounce

Massage onto lower abdomen and back.

Amenorrhea and Irregular Cycles, Formula 2

Yarrow, 3 drops

Clary sage, 8 drops

Chamomile, 6 drops

Carrier oil, 1 ounce

Massage onto lower abdomen and back.

PMS Fluid–Retention Bath

Juniper, 4 drops

Lavender, 2 drops

Add to bath water after the tub is full.

PMS Antitension Blend

Neroli, 7 drops
Ylang-ylang, 3 drops
Clary sage, 5 drops
Carrier oil, 1 ounce

Massage onto abdomen or chest as needed.

PMS Good Mood Bath

Neroli, 2 drops
Clary sage, 2 drops
Ylang-ylang, 2 drops

Mix with a handful of sea salt. Add to bath water.

PMS-Related Painful Breasts

Geranium, 5 milliliters
Carrier oil, 50 milliliters

Massage onto breasts before and during menstruation
as needed.

Migraine Headache with Periods, Compress Treatment

Peppermint or lavender, 3 to 4 drops

Bowl of cool water

Add essential oils to water, dip in a cloth, wring out, and apply to head. When the cloth warms, repeat.

Menopause Formula

Neroli, 6 drops

Mandarin, 3 drops

Clary sage, 2 drops

Carrier oil, 1 ounce

Massage the solar plexus (the area below the ribcage in the center of the chest) in a clockwise direction.

Cleopatra's Aphrodisiac Blend

Jasmine or ylang-ylang, 4 drops

Rose, 3 drops

Neroli, 1 drop

Carrier oil, ¾ ounce

Anoint pulse points and wear as a perfume.

Treating
Children's Ailments
with Aromatherapy

B y using aromatherapy as a natural remedy for your children's ailments, you can provide comfort and healing without the worry of the unknown side effects and chemical additives of over-the-counter medications. Lavender sitz baths can rapidly heal a baby's diaper rash. Cider vinegar and lavender compresses can speed the healing of swollen, bruised knees. A bottle of tea tree oil can save the day when mosquitoes attack during an outing.

Children's natural vigor and powerful immune systems make them highly responsive to aromatherapy. A little help from nature is often all that's needed to jump-start the body's own defenses. Natural remedies are safest and most effective at the beginning of an illness, which is why it's important to be tuned in to the first sign of ill health before the condition becomes serious.

To equip your aromatherapy medicine chest, have on hand amber dropper bottles, a selection of the most useful essential oils (see "Essential Oils for Children's Ailments," below), a carrier oil such as almond or grapeseed, flannels for compresses (cloth diapers work well, too), and an aromatherapy diffuser or lamp. All these items are available at most health–food stores.

ESSENTIAL OILS FOR CHILDREN'S AILMENTS

ESSENTIAL OIL	AILMENTS
Tea tree	First aid, bug bites, bug repellent, anti-infectious, all-purpose
Lavender	First aid, sunburn, anti-infectious, all-purpose
Peppermint	Fevers, digestive
Eucalyptus[1]	Respiratory, fevers
Sandalwood	Sore throats, sedative
Chamomile	Calming, digestive, ear infections, all-purpose
Bergamot	Viruses, fevers
Mandarin, grapefruit, orange	Mood-enhancing
St. John's wort (usually sold in an herbal oil form)	Ear infections

[1]Use in low dosage.

DOSAGE AND SAFETY

Always use essential oils diluted in a carrier oil (the exceptions to this rule are tea tree and lavender, which can be used neat). Reduce dosages and formulas intended for adults by half or more, depending on the child's body weight and constitution. For very young children, this means 1 to 3 drops of essential oil to 1 ounce of carrier oil. (See chapters 4 and 9.)

Start by having your child sniff the oil—if the child sneezes or seems to dislike the oil, don't use it. To determine if your child is highly sensitive or allergic, do a patch test: Mix a few drops of carrier oil with the essential oil in the palm of your hand, rub it on a small area of the child's skin, cover it with a bandage, and observe after twenty-four hours. If redness, itchiness, or a rash develops, don't use it. A very sensitive child may still be able to use lavender and chamomile. If any condition becomes serious, consult a medical doctor.

103

INFANT AILMENTS

Diaper rash is often the result of yeast overgrowth. *Candida albicans*, a natural microorganism that inhabits our bodies, often gets out of control in moist body folds. A daily lavender sitz bath can rapidly eliminate *Candida* and soothe the irritation. Add 1 to 3 drops of lavender oil to a sink or small tub filled to the baby's hip with tepid water, and agitate the water to disperse the oil. Sit baby in the tub for five to fifteen minutes. Sprinkle natural baby powder on baby's skin after the bath to keep the folds of skin dry, but avoid cornstarch because it may aggravate diaper rash.

Chamomile is beneficial for teething. It soothes the pain and calms baby's nerves. Prepare a massage blend with 1 ounce of carrier oil and 6 drops of chamomile. Warm the oil in your hand, or place the container in warm water. Massage the blend along baby's jaw and around the ears. If your baby's not sleeping well because of teething distress, try adding 1 drop of chamomile oil to a warm-water bath before bed.

FIRST AID FOR CHILDREN

A family picnic at the beach? A hike in the woods? No backpack is complete without a bottle of tea tree or lavender oil. Useful as wound cleansers, insect repellents, and painkillers, these essences are virtual medicine chests in a bottle.

Wounds

Make a wound cleanser by adding 1 part tea tree oil to 10 parts water. Shake vigorously, then wash the wound. Even when you're out in the woods and no sanitary facility is available, this mixture is an effective disinfectant.

Insect Bites

Lavender oil is immediately effective in relieving the sting or itch of insect bites. For bites and stings, you can use the oil neat or undiluted. Dab the lavender directly onto the bite as needed. For an insect repellent, fill a 4-ounce spray bottle with 3 ounces of water and 1 ounce of aloe vera juice or witch hazel, then add 24 drops of tea tree oil. Shake before use. For older kids, double the amount of tea tree oil in the mix.

Burns

Lavender oil has been known to heal burns. Apply undiluted for emergency care of burns. For sunburn, add 6 drops of lavender to a basin of cool water. Dip a flannel or diaper into the basin to pick up the film of oil on the water, and apply it to the skin until the child's skin temperature drops. For a soothing bath, add 6 to 10 drops of lavender to a lukewarm tub and have the child soak. Mix 4 ounces of aloe vera gel with 20 drops of lavender, shake well, and gently apply to the sunburn when the child gets out.

105

Bruises

For those unavoidable skinned knees and bruises, use compresses. Fill a bowl with equal parts cool water and apple cider vinegar, and pour in 6 drops of lavender. Dip in a diaper or flannel, wring out the excess liquid, and apply to the bruised area. When the flannel warms, repeat the procedure. Once the heat and swelling have subsided, gently massage the bruise with a blend of 1 ounce of carrier oil with 3 drops of chamomile, 3 drops of lavender, and 1 drop of lemon oil (an optional anti-inflammatory). Massage this mix into affected area two to three times a day until the injury is healed.

CHILDHOOD CONDITIONS

Ear Infections

Chronic ear infections are a relatively recent phenomenon in young children who are overexposed to drug therapy and who develop resistance to antibiotics, lowered immunity, and yeast overgrowth. Mainstream medicine treats these conditions with yet more drugs. Natural remedies can help prevent this vicious cycle.

At the onset of ear trouble, make a mixture of 3 drops of chamomile to a bowl of hot water, and apply a compress as warm as is comfortable over the ear. Reapply a new compress as it cools, adding more chamomile oil as needed. Next, dab a cotton ball with the following blend: 3 drops of chamomile, 3 drops of lavender, and 1 ounce of carrier oil. Gently place the cotton ball in the ear, replacing it with a fresh cotton ball three times a day. Follow this regime until the infection is gone.

Daily eucalyptus inhalations will loosen mucus and fight infection. To steaming water, add 3 drops of eucalyptus oil. Have the child inhale the steam with a towel covering her head. To fight internal infections, garlic capsules taken daily by mouth are helpful. If your child is prone to ear infections, try a massage with St. John's wort herbal oil for maintenance care.

For a few months after any ear infection, massage the child's neck one to three times a week along the lymph chain (in the hollow under the ear, along the pulse in the neck, and down to the hollow above the collarbone).

An ear infection can be a serious condition. Consult a health-care practitioner to monitor your child's progress.

Colds, Flus, and Fevers

Colds and flus seem to be a given during the school year, but you can take preventive measures against these and other contagious diseases. Add 2 drops of eucalyptus or tea tree oil to the bath water each time you bathe your child. Cleanse and purify the air while he sleeps by adding 6 to 8 drops of eucalyptus oil to a diffuser or warm-air vaporizer.

At the first sign of flu symptoms, put your child in a moderately hot bath to which you've added 3 to 6 drops of tea tree oil, then straight into a warm bed (Davis 1988). Peppermint and eucalyptus are both very cooling oils and are indicated for fever. (Use only 1 drop of peppermint oil at a time, as too much can be stimulating.) To cool a fever, add 1 to 3 drops of peppermint oil to a bowl of cool water, and apply with a sponge or forehead compress. (Don't use peppermint oil on irritated skin.) For a respiratory infection, put the child in a full bath with 3 to 6 drops of eucalyptus oil in the water. For a sore throat, use a steam inhalation with eucalyptus oil.

A warm massage is very comforting when a child is sick with the flu or a chest cold. To 1 ounce of carrier oil, add 2 drops of lavender, 1 to 2 drops of eucalyptus, and 2 drops of chamomile. Gently massage the areas of most discomfort. To loosen mucus, rub the child's chest with this formula, moving from the middle of her chest out toward her armpits. In addition to relieving discomfort, the anti-infectious properties of these oils can help your child get well.

For a tummy ache, tuck the child into bed, massage the tummy with 1 ounce of carrier oil to 4 drops of chamomile, and cover with a warm flannel and hot water bottle or heating pad.

Chicken Pox and Measles

Antiviral essential oils such as eucalyptus and bergamot can help your child get over chicken pox quickly. Bathe the child in luke-warm water with 2 drops of tea tree oil, 2 drops of bergamot, and 2 drops of eucalyptus. To stop itching, make a lotion of 2 ounces of witch hazel and 2 ounces of water. Add 5 drops each of lavender, chamomile, and tea tree oil. Shake well and dab on as needed.

For the measles, continuously diffuse or vaporize eucalyptus in the child's room to alleviate the respiratory problems that usually accompany this illness. To reduce fever, give the child a sponge bath every few hours with bergamot or chamomile.

"Party-Time Moods"

Preparty jitters and excitement can be overwhelming for children. Calm overstimulated children with mandarin, grapefruit, or orange essential oil added to an aromatherapy diffuser. Make a little girl's perfume from equal parts mandarin and sandalwood, and dab behind the ears and at the nape of the neck. When the party's over and the kids refuse to go to bed, wind them down in a bath with 3 drops of sandalwood oil and 3 drops of lavender oil. If too many treats have brought on a tummy ache, use the belly rub formula on page 107 in the "Colds, Flus, and Fevers" section.

8

Beauty Care

Care of the skin is part of overall health maintenance. Taking steps to rejuvenate ourselves creates a physical and mental resiliency that better enables us to withstand the stress of the modern world. Natural substances in beauty care work harmoniously with the structure of the skin. Aromatic oils enhance the protective quality of the epidermis without disturbing the integrity of the skin surface. Essential oils interact with the chemistry of the skin and act on skin metabolism, increasing circulation and bringing deeper oxygenation to the skin tissues. The increased circulation in the dermis layer of the skin has a direct effect on lymph and blood flow, aiding in the removal of waste and toxins, eliminating blemishes, and increasing overall health. The same regenerative property that enables essential oils to regenerate skin tissue and aid the healing of scars and wounds makes them useful in treating wrinkles and age-related skin conditions.

Natural home facial therapy not only introduces these natural biological substances that nourish the skin, but also stimulates touch receptors, toning muscle tissue, regenerating skin, and creating an antistress response.

ESSENTIAL OILS FOR SKIN THERAPY

Skin Condition	Essential Oils
Oily skin or acne	Ylang-ylang, lavender, tea tree, thyme, lemon, niaouli, cajeput, juniper, geranium
Dry skin	Neroli, rose, geranium, clary sage, jasmine, carrot seed, petitgrain, mandarin, palmarosa
Wrinkles and devitalized skin	Frankincense, rockrose, neroli, geranium, clary sage, carrot seed, myrrh
Sensitive skin	Chamomile (German or Roman), *Helichrysum italicum,* neroli, rose, angelica, carrot seed, palmarosa
Couperose (broken capillaries)	German chamomile, *Helichrysum italicum,* rosemary verbenone, lemon

---

Having a well-balanced lifestyle that includes setting aside time every week for self-nurturing relieves stress and enhances our overall health and well-being. Just as the glow of healthy skin reflects good internal health, negative mental attitudes and extreme external stress affect the functioning of body systems. External stress may at times be beyond our ability to control. Areas of our lives that we can influence include developing a positive mental attitude, eating nourishing foods, and getting adequate exercise, sunshine, fresh air, and self-care—including beauty care.

NATURAL FACIAL TREATMENTS

For a natural, do-it-yourself facial treatment, follow these steps:

1. Steam the skin with essential oils and chamomile.
2. Apply the appropriate mask for your skin type. Place tea bags over eyes.
3. Apply aromatic hydrosol or tonic to the face and neck.
4. Massage in the essential oil blend for your skin type.
5. Apply moisturizer to the undereye area, neck, and dry areas on the face.

111

Facial Steam

Boil a quart of water, then lower to a simmer and add 2 tablespoons of chamomile herb. Turn off the heat and add 2 drops of lavender and 3 drops of rosemary. Cover your head and the pot with a towel and let the aromatic vapors penetrate your facial skin. Steam for 5 or 10 minutes.

Spot Treatment Lotion for Oily or Blemished Skin

Baking soda, ¼ teaspoon

Water, ½ cup

Mix well. Apply to blackheads or blemishes with a cotton ball. Use this treatment after the steam and before you apply the mask.

Mask Therapies

Clay Masks

Clay masks are used in beauty therapy to draw out impurities. Clays have the ability to absorb toxins as they are eliminated from skin. In clay mask treatment, the heat under the layer of clay is increased by trapped body heat, causing pore-cleansing perspiration. Clays also remineralize skin tissues; minerals are a necessary component of skin health. Clays contain necessary minerals like silica, aluminum, iron, calcium, magnesium, sodium, potassium, and trace elements. Without mineral salts, skin loses moisture and becomes devitalized and sagging.

To draw out impurities, let the mask dry until it gets tight. Avoid leaving the mask on too long, because it can be drying to the skin. To remove the mask, soak a small towel in tepid water, wrap around the face, and allow the mask to moisten. Then gently wipe off the mask.

Thalassotherapy Masks

Thalassotherapy is a term used for health therapy with seaweed (algae), sea plants, and seawater. Thalassotherapy is very popular in European health spas, where treatments using seaweed are given for conditions such as aches and pains, arthritis, and cellulite (fatty deposits on the thighs and buttocks). Seaweed contains iodine, a mineral necessary for the proper function of the thyroid gland, which regulates metabolism, body heat, and the rate at which we store and burn fat—hence thalassotherapy's success in treating cellulite.

Thalassotherapy is used in many types of beauty treatments, including treatments for the face and skin, because these sea elements are such a rich source of nutrients. The most commonly used varieties of seaweed are *Fucus vesiculosis* (kelp), *Laminaria* (brown algae), and chondria, which contain iodine, amino acids, alginic acids, polysaccharides, magnesium, potassium, calcium, and vitamins A, D, B, and C. Algaes also contain the trace elements lithium and vanadium, which tone the nervous system and aid in stress reduction. The chemical composition of seawater and sea plants is very similar to that of human blood plasma. This similarity makes them an ideal source of beneficial minerals and vitamins. Using seaweed in combination with essential oils is extremely effective, because essential oils facilitate skin penetration of the ions and nutrients contained in the seaweed.

Seaweeds have the ability to hold a great deal of moisture, so when using them in your home beauty preparations, remember that only a small quantity is needed; the seaweed expands when water is added. Kelp powder is readily available at most

113

health-food stores. *Caution:* If you have hyperthyroidism, consult with a health professional before using seaweeds.

Papaya Masks

Papaya enzymes dissolve and exfoliate rough dry skin from the surface of the epidermis. The result is smoother skin with a finer texture. The removal of dead surface cells allows deeper penetration of essential oils and moisture. All skin types benefit from papaya, particularly dehydrated, sun-damaged, unevenly textured, or wrinkled skin.

Egg Mask for Dry Skin

Yolk of 1 egg
Hazelnut oil, ½ teaspoon
Geranium, 3 drops

Slightly beat egg yolk and stir in other ingredients. Apply to face and neck. Leave on for 20 to 30 minutes.

Clay Mask for Oily, Blemished, or Congested Skin

Green clay, 1½ teaspoons
Grapeseed oil, ⅓ teaspoon
Tea tree, 3 drops

Combine ingredients and add enough water or hydrosol to make a creamy paste. Leave on for 15 minutes.

Seaweed Mask for Devitalized or Wrinkled Skin

Kelp powder, 1½ teaspoons

Wheat germ oil, ½ teaspoon

Frankincense, 2 drops

Peppermint, 1 drop

Combine ingredients and add enough hydrosol or water to bring to a creamy consistency. Apply to skin and leave on for 20 to 30 minutes.

115

Papaya Mask for Exfoliation and Smooth Skin

1 papaya

Honey, ½ teaspoon

Bergamot, 3 drops

Mash the papaya to a smooth consistency, and mix in the other ingredients. Apply to face and neck. Leave on for 20 to 30 minutes. Massage into skin, then rinse with cool water.

Treatment for Puffy Eyes

Thoroughly wet 2 tea bags of black tea with cold water. Apply 1 to each eye during mask treatments.

Postmask Aromatic Tonic

Apple cider vinegar, ¼ ounce

Pure water, 7¾ ounces

Yarrow, 14 drops

Mix ingredients. Shake before using. Apply to face and neck using a cotton ball after mask treatments.

Beauty Blends

116

Each essential oil has a unique therapeutic effect (see the table on page 110). Your personal blend can be customized for your individual beauty needs. To blend your own facial or body oil, use 1 ounce of carrier to 7 to 10 drops of the appropriate essential oils.

Carrier Oils for Beauty Blends

Choose from the following vegetable oils to make your beauty blends: grapeseed, hazelnut, apricot kernel, avocado, rosehip, and macadamia nut. Wheat germ oil has a high vitamin E content and can be added to any blend to enrich its antioxidant properties.

Massage one of the following blends into the skin after mask treatments.

Rose Blend for Dry Skin

Rose, 5 drops

Rosehip seed oil, ½ ounce

Apricot kernel oil, ½ ounce

Blend for Devitalized or Wrinkled Skin

Frankincense, 8 drops

Rockrose, 2 drops

Hazelnut oil, 1 ounce

Wheat germ oil, 1 teaspoon

117

Blend for Sensitive Skin or Couperose Skin (Broken Capillaries)

Roman chamomile, 3 drops

German chamomile, 6 drops

Yarrow, 2 drops

Rosemary verbenone, 1 drop

Hazelnut oil, 1 ounce

Wheat germ oil, 2 teaspoons

HEALING WITH AROMATHERAPY

Blend for Oily Skin

Ylang-ylang, 7 drops
Lavender, 3 drops
Grapeseed oil, 1 ounce

BEAUTY BATHS

Create an antistress environment for your beauty bath. Dim the lights and light a candle. Brew a cup of melissa or chamomile tea. Play soothing classical music.

Choose a recipe from those listed below, and add to the bath just before you get in to receive the full benefit of the vapors.

Cleopatra Milk Bath for Dehydrated Skin

Neroli blossom, 3 drops
Mandarin, 3 drops
Milk, 1 cup

Add to bath water.

Soothing Skin Bath for Sensitive Skin or Skin with Broken Capillaries

    Chamomile (German or Roman), 4 drops

    Lavender, 2 drops

    Yolk of 1 egg

Add to bath water.

Bath for Fluid Retention or Edema

    Rosemary, 2 drops

    Juniper, 4 drops

    Lavender, 2 drops

    Sea salt, 2 cups

Add to bath water.

119

OTHER BODY TREATMENTS

Detox Sauna Treatment

Eucalyptus, 3 drops

Pine, 3 drops

Water, 1 cup

Mix together and gently pour on the sauna stones (be careful not to splatter yourself with essential oils). After the sauna, rinse with cool water and apply the following lymph blend to encourage the removal of wastes.

Lymph Support Blend

Bay laurel, 6 drops

Lavender, 4 drops

Grapeseed oil, 1 ounce

Apply to lymph nodes on the sides of the neck, in the hollows between the jaw and ear and at the collarbone, and at the top of the thigh along the groin.

Aromatic Shower

To benefit from essential oils in a quick and easy way, apply 3 or 4 drops of essential oil to a washcloth and massage over the body. Choose an oil appropriate to your health condition. For example, if you are suffering from nasal congestion, choose eucalyptus; for poor circulation, choose rosemary; for fluid retention, choose juniper; for depression, choose mandarin; for anxiety, choose clary sage; and for insomnia, choose neroli.

Rosemary Oil Detoxification Brushing Treatment

Apply 1 or 2 drops of rosemary oil to a natural-bristle back brush. In the shower, gently brush with upward strokes, starting from the feet, working toward the neck in the direction of the lymph flow. This treatment stimulates the lymph and blood flow and encourages the disposal of bodily waste. If you have allergic or sensitive skin, do not use this treatment.

121

Body Beautiful Oil

Clary sage, 20 drops

Lavender, 10 drops

Grapeseed oil, 2 ounces

Apricot kernel oil, 2 ounces

Wheat germ oil, 1 teaspoon

Apply to moist skin after bathing.

Cellulite Oil

Cypress, 5 drops

Rosemary, 3 drops

Juniper, 3 drops

Fennel, 4 drops

Avocado oil, 1 ounce

Massage into affected area with upward circular strokes until the oil is absorbed.

Cellulite Bath

Powdered kelp, ½ cup

Sea salt, ½ cup

Cypress, 4 drops

Juniper, 4 drops

Add the kelp and salt as you run the hot water. Just before you get in, add the essential oils.

HAIR CARE

Incorporating aromatherapy into your hair-care regime results in beautiful, luxurious hair. Essential oils can be added to any natural hair product to enhance its effectiveness. Rosemary oil has traditionally been used to stimulate hair growth by increasing circulation in the scalp. Lemon and geranium are used to dissolve sebaceous deposits that clog follicles in oily hair. Chamomile conditions dry or delicate hair.

Rosemary Hair Treatment

Rosemary, 6 drops
Lavender, 6 drops
Jojoba oil, 1 ounce

Moisten hair, then massage oil into scalp for at least 3 minutes. Focus your massage on the back of the head above the neck to improve blood flow into the scalp area. Wrap hair in plastic, then wrap a towel over the plastic. Leave on for 20 to 30 minutes, then shampoo.

123

Shampoo for Dry Hair

Chamomile, 8 drops
Neroli, 5 drops
Grapeseed oil, ½ teaspoon
Shampoo, 8-ounce bottle

Mix together and shake before using.

Shampoo for Oily Hair

Lemon, 8 drops
Geranium, 8 drops
Shampoo, 8-ounce bottle

Mix together and shake before using.

Alopecia
(Balding)

In a recent randomized study, eighty-four male and female volunteers with alopecia areata were given placebo treatment or essential oils (thyme, rosemary, cedar, and lavender in a base of grapeseed or jojoba). The oil mixture was applied daily with at least two minutes of scalp massage, followed by a warm towel application. There was significant improvement in the essential oil group. Researchers noted that the topical application of aromatics benefits alopecia patients without the toxicity and serious side effects of the drug therapies often used to treat this condition.

Alopecia Treatment

Rosemary and lavender, 3 parts
Thyme and cedarwood, 2 parts

Add to a base of jojoba and grapeseed oil. Massage into the scalp for at least 2 minutes per day, followed by a warm towel application. Allow several months for results.

9

Safety and Toxicity
of Essential Oils

Botanical medicines and essential oils are extremely safe in comparison to conventional medicines. In 1998, over one million cases of toxic exposure to pharmaceuticals were reported to poison control centers; 898 of those cases resulted in death. The largest number of deaths occurred from such commonly used drugs as analgesics, cardiovascular drugs, antihistamines, and asthma drugs. Over seventy thousand cases had problematic outcomes listed as moderate to major. In contrast, only 4,066 cases of toxic exposure to essential oils were reported. None of those resulted in death, and the vast majority of problematic outcomes were listed as none or minor.

Dosage is an important factor that can determine whether use of an essential oil is safe. When used in the standard 2 to 2.5 percent dilution recommended by holistic aromatherapists, essential oils are safe. At a low dose and for a short duration of time, even oils that are considered moderately toxic can be used safely. (Remember, however, that toxic oils should only be used under the supervision of a knowledgeable professional.)

TOXICITY

Toxicity refers to the degree to which a substance is poisonous, and depends on dosage. (For a list of oils with varying levels and types of toxicity, see the accompanying table.) Acute toxicity occurs after a single dose. Chronic toxicity occurs with long-term use (weeks, months, or years). Over the years, only a few deaths have occurred worldwide from the ingestion of essential oils. Other toxic effects from overconsumption of essential oils have included serious liver dysfunction and severe stomach upset. In the cases of liver dysfunction, total recovery was achieved.

Oral Toxicity

Oral toxicity data are based on animal testing and come from the cosmetics industry. The standard evaluation system is the LD-50, which stands for "lethal dose 50 percent," meaning that a single dose of a given substance proved fatal for 50 percent of the test animals (usually mice). These data do not always translate accurately to human physiology, but do give an indication of toxicity.

Over-the-counter medications such as aspirin have a higher potential for oral toxicity than do the majority of essential oils commonly used in aromatherapy. Large quantities of the oils—a cup or more of most—would have to be consumed to prove fatal. For a small percentage of essential oils, however, fatality is possible from ingestion of only 5 milliters (1 teaspoon) or 10 milliliters. A child died after ingestion of 5 milliliters of *Eucalyptus globulus*, for instance, although the LD-50 for a lethal dose for a child was indicated to be 34 milliliters. Many variables enter into how an essential oil will affect an individual, including chemical variability, possible adulterants, and constitutional weakness such as liver or kidney deficiencies (Schnaubelt 1998; Sheppard-Hanger 1995).

Neurotoxicity

Ketones in high quantities can be neurotoxic (i.e., poisonous to the brain) and may induce an epileptic episode. Not all essential oils containing ketones are dangerous. Fenchone in fennel oil is considered nontoxic, yet carvone in dill is considered toxic. Carvone is also present in caraway and spearmint, but not in sufficient quantities to be harmful, and both oils are considered safe. Rosemary and peppermint contain the ketones camphor and menthone and are safe when used at therapeutic low doses. Peppermint should be used with caution by small children. Poisonous ketone-containing oils that should be avoided completely are mugwort, santolina, rue, pennyroyal, and wormwood (Schnaubelt 1998).

127

Thujone is also a toxic constituent, although not all essential oils containing it are unsafe. This variation in toxicity may be due to the four molecular shapes of the thujone molecule, which may each act differently on a physiologic level. Thujone is found in sage, mugwort, thuja, wormwood, and yarrow. Sage oil has moderate toxicity and when used with caution is safe. Yarrow has minimal toxicity and when used with caution is safe; however, it

TOXICITY OF ESSENTIAL OILS

LEVEL OF TOXICITY	ESSENTIAL OILS
Hazardous: *Avoid completely*	Mugwort, mustard, horseradish, tansy, goosefoot, savin, pennyroyal, rue, calamus, boldo, bitter almond, wormseed, wormwood
Very toxic: *Avoid*	Cornmint, sassafras, ajowan, buchu, jaborandi, turpentine, tonka bean, wintergreen, thuja
Toxic:[1] *Low dosage* *with caution*	Wintergreen,[2] thuja,[2] savory,[2] sweet birch,[2] oregano, myrrh, hyssop, basil, birch, clove leaf, bay leaf, tarragon, sage, thyme, nutmeg, arnica
Skin sensitization: *May cause allergic* *reaction*	Clove leaf, cinnamon bark, cinnamon leaves, *Cassia,* oregano, thyme, savory, costus, elecampane, Tolu balsam, Peru balsam
Phototoxic: *Strong to moderate*	RUTACEAE FAMILY: bergamot, bitter orange, rue, lemon, lime UMBELLIFERAE FAMILY: angelica root, cumin, opopanax, *Ammi visnaga,* tarragon, *Tagetes,* celery, parsley VERBENACEAE FAMILY: verbena
Considered safe but *not for children*	Aniseed, bay laurel
Considered safe but *not during pregnancy*	Aniseed, marjoram, cedarwood atlas (*Cedrus atlantica*), spearmint

LEVEL OF TOXICITY	ESSENTIAL OILS
Considered safe with cautions for external use	
Possible skin sensitization	Benzoin, *Litsea cubeba,* peppermint, pine, (*pinus sylvestris*), yarrow, ylang-ylang
Possible mild skin sensitization	Fir
Possible moderate to mild phototoxicity	Lavandin, lavender (*L. angustifolium,* spike, *L. latifolia*), lemongreass, orange (sweet, *Citrus aurantium*), mandarin, grapefruit
Considered safe with low toxicity	Cajuput, cananga, caraway, cardamom, carrot seed, chamomile (German and Roman), *Cistus ladaniferous,* clary sage, coriander, cubeb (*piper cubeba*), cypress, elemi, eucalyptus[3], sweet fennel, frankincense, galbanum, geranium, jasmin, juniper berry[4], neroli, patchouli, pepper (black), petitgrain (orange leaf, *Citrus aurantium*), rose, rosemary, rosewood, sandalwood, tangerine, tea tree, vetiver

129

[1] Essential oils listed as toxic are commonly used by professional aromatherapists.

[2] These oils do have potential for greater toxicity, especially thuja, savory, and wintergreen.

[3] Use low dose for children.

[4] Not for internal use.

Note: Use caution and common sense (low dose, short term, and only under the direction of a knowledgeable professional) when using these oils. These lists do not include every essential oil that may become available on the aromatherapy market. Always use proper dosage guidelines for any essential oil. Check with a knowledgeable professional before using untested or unknown oils.

should be avoided by children. Essential oils containing thujone should be avoided by pregnant women and children.

Caution is advised for the following oils, which have neurotoxic and abortive effects:

Hyssop (pinocamphone)—External use only
Lavandula stoechas (camphor)—Never use with children
Thuja (thujone)—Generally nonproblematic when
used at low doses; for external use only

Liver Toxicity

130

Essential oils that contain the chemical constituent phenol can be toxic to the liver; long-term use even at low dosages can lead to changes in liver enzyme counts. Phenols are used in aromatherapy for their antibacterial properties. Essential oils that contain phenols, such as thyme and oregano, are often recommended by aromatherapists to fight infectious conditions. A safe and effective limit for internal use in adults is two to four days at a dosage of 3 drops three times a day. Children and pregnant and lactating women should not use it. Clove and savory also contain phenols; their use should be avoided because of possible irritation to skin and mucous membranes (Schnaubelt 1998).

Kidney Toxicity
(Nephrotoxicity)

Essential oil of juniper has traditionally been used for kidney disorders. The stimulating effect of juniper on the kidneys, however, is actually a result of irritation; monoterpenes are the chemical constituents responsible for this irritant effect. Juniper should be used with caution and is not recommended for internal use. Only essential oil extracted from the berry, rather than from other parts of the plant, should be used at all; juniper berry oil contains terpene alcohols and only minute amounts of monoterpenes. *Juniperus sabina* is said to be toxic to the kidneys even when applied externally.

Essential oils that contain methyl salicylate can also be toxic to the kidneys in high doses; these include sweet birch (*Betula lenta*) and wintergreen (*Gaultheria procumbens*). Sassafras oil, a hazardous essence not used in aromatherapy, is also toxic to the kidneys.

131

EXTERNAL APPLICATION: SKIN REACTIONS

Sensitization (Allergic Reaction)

Skin sensitization is an allergic reaction that may result in rash, irritation, blotches, redness, itching, and blistering. More severe symptoms may also occur, such as contact dermatitis, swelling, and shortness of breath. Symptoms can occur after a one-time application or from repeated applications. The constituent cinnamic aldehyde, a strong sensitizing agent, is found in cinnamon and cassia. A few cases of sensitization have been reported from clove bud and ylang-ylang oils.

Other possible sensitizers are massoia, laurel, and *Inula graveolens*. The terpenes in these pine oils have been blamed for sensitization. It has been found, however, that it is not the terpene content that is responsible for skin reactions, but rather the terpene hydroperoxides that result from improper storage and manufacturing of these oils (Tisserand 1985; Schnaubelt 1998; Sheppard-Hanger 1995).

Persons who are prone to eczema, dermatitis, or psoriasis are especially vulnerable to skin reactions. Individuals with sensitive skin may react to such commonly used essential oils as geranium or Scotch pine. A patch test can be used to determine possible reactions: Place a few drops of essential oil in the bend of the arm and leave on for twenty-four hours. Repeat this procedure again after forty-eight hours. If reactions occur, do not use the oil.

Phototoxicity

132

Photosensitivity is a skin reaction that occurs after application of a substance with subsequent exposure to ultraviolet light from sunlight or a tanning booth. Symptoms are inflammation and redness, which subside in three days. Photoallergy is characterized by dermatitis or burns. Photocarcinogenesis is a more serious condition in which a skin cancer is induced by long-term exposure to ultraviolet light in combination with a phototoxic substance. The essential oil constituents believed responsible for this condition are furocoumarins, bergaptene, and xanthotoxin (methoxypsoralen). The primary plant families that may cause phototoxic reactions are Rutaceae, Umbelliferae, and Verbenaceae (Tisserand 1985; Sheppard-Hanger 1995).

CONTRAINDICATIONS AND ILLNESS

Avoid certain essential oils if you have any of the conditions listed in the accompanying table.

CONTRAINDICATIONS FOR ESSENTIAL OILS

Condition	Essential Oils to Avoid
Asthma	Camphor, marjoram, oregano, rosemary, yarrow
Breast, uterine, and ovarian cancers	Cypress, angelica, sage, fennel, anise, caraway
Digestive problems, ulcers	Clove, cinnamon, oregano, parsley seed
Epilepsy	Anise, fennel, hyssop, nutmeg, sage, parsley, thuja, wintergreen
Glaucoma	Cypress, hyssop, thyme, tarragon
Hemorrhage[1]	Lavender, tonka bean
Hypertension	Hyssop, lemon
Hypothyroidism	Catnip,[2] black spruce,[2] fennel[2]
Insomnia	Peppermint, pine
Prostate cancer	Angelica, cypress, hyssop, *thymus serpyllum*
Tumors	Anise, caraway, fennel
Urinary tract infection and kidney disease	Black pepper, eucalyptus, juniper, opopanax, parsley seed

133

[1] While using anticoagulant medication, avoid coumarin-containing essential oils because they may cause hemorrhage.

[2] Avoid if you are on thyroid medication or have hypothyroidism.

PREGNANCY AND CHILDREN

Women who are pregnant or lactating should consult a physician before using any essential oil. Refer to the safe-with-low-toxicity oils in the table on page 129, which have been tested for safety.

To find oils appropriate for children, parents may choose from the same safe-with-low-toxicity list. Always dilute the oils and use according to appropriate guidelines.

Children and pregnant or lactating women should avoid all essential oils listed as hazardous, very toxic, toxic, sensitizing, and phototoxic on pages 128–129.

ESSENTIAL OILS IN PREGNANCY

DEGREE OF SAFETY	ESSENTIAL OILS
Abortive (avoid during pregnancy)	Mugwort, pennyroyal, thuja, wormwood, savin, tansy, rue
Contraindicated in pregnancy (avoid during pregnancy)	Ajowan, bitter almond, basil, bay leaf, sweet birch, buchu, clove leaf, clove stem, cornmint, davana (Artemisia pallens), hyssop, marjoram, myrrh, oregano, sage, savory, tarragon, thyme (all types)
Questionable (avoid during pregnancy)	Aniseed, parsley seed, cedarwood (atlas, Cedrus atlantica), Tagetes, spearmint, camphor
Safe at low dose during pregnancy	Mandarin, petitgrain, sandalwood, jasmin, ylang-ylang, patchouli
Considered safe during pregnancy	Chamomile, geranium, lavender, rose, neroli

10

Aromatic
Plant Families

Plants are divided into groups called families. Each family has certain identifying physical characteristics. Aromatic plants are dominant in only a small percentage of plant families; from these families several hundred essential oils are extracted, of which only about eighty are used in aromatherapy.

Medicinal properties of plants often fall into familial groups. In this chapter, we will discuss only a few of the medicinal plant families that contain important aromatic plants.

LAMIACEAE

The Lamiaceae family produces more essential oils than any other. It contains about 5,600 species and 224 genera, including many important medicinal and culinary plants. Their main areas of distribution are in tropical and warmer temperate regions. These plants are easy to identify by their common family characteristics: herbs and small shrubs with square stems bearing minute oil glands that dot the usually opposite (or sometimes whorled) leaves. They usually have some flowers or spikelets (called axils) toward the top of the stem. The oil glands on the leaves are the source of the volatile oils used in aromatherapy.

Some of the plants in the Lamiaceae family have been used as medicinal herbs for thousands of years. Plants in the Lamiaceae family are antiseptic, antispasmodic, and sudorific and tend to be tonic and energizing. They have an affinity for the respiratory system and many are digestive aids. Many of these oils have analgesic and anti-inflammative properties, making them helpful for treating headaches, congestion, and muscular aches and pains.

The majority of plants in this botanical family are therapeutically safe. The chemical constituents in the Lamiaceae family that have potential for toxicity are ketones in pennyroyal and sage, and phenols in basil, oregano, savory, and thyme.

The genus *Salvia* (sages) contains more than 900 species, including many medicinals. This genus has an affinity for the reproductive system and is used therapeutically for female reproductive system disorders such as leukorrhea.

Aromatic medicinal plant members of the Lamiaceae family include hyssop (*Hyssopus officinalis*), lavender (*Lavandula officinalis, vera,* and *stoechas*), spike lavender (*Lavandula latifolia*), lemon balm (*Melissa officinalis*), peppermint (*Mentha piperita*), spearmint (*Mentha spicata*), bee balm (*Monarda species*), catnip (*Nepeta cataria*), basil (*Ocimum basilicum*), holy basil (*Ocimum sanctum*), oregano (*Origanum*), marjoram (*Majorana hortensis, Origanum majorana*), patchouli (*Pogostemon heyneanus*), rosemary (*Rosmarinus officinalis*), sage (*Salvia officinalis*), clary sage (*Salvia sclarea*), savory (*Satureja montana, S. hortensis*), and many varieties of thyme (*Thymus vulgaris*).

MYRTACEAE

The Myrtaceae family contains about 3,850 species and 121 genera. Many plants of this family are important for timber production. Their primary areas of distribution are in tropical, subtropical, and warm regions—primarily Australia and tropical America. The Myrtaceae consist mainly of shrubs and trees with thick, glandular, evergreen, opposite leaves dotted with oil glands on a woody plant with feathery, showy flowers (eucalyptus and myrtle have handsome tufts of long stamens); the fruit is a woody capsule or berry. The oil glands in the leaves contain the volatile oils used in aromatherapy.

137

Plants of the Myrtaceae family are strongly antiseptic, astringent, expectorant, and tonic, with antiviral properties. The Myrtaceae have an affinity for the respiratory system, especially the lungs. There are also many culinary uses for members of this family; for instance, allspice from *Pimenta*, cloves from *Eugenia aromatica*, and jellies from the *psidium* species.

Eugenol is the common constituent in allspice and clove. Clove is potentially toxic and can cause skin sensitization. Niaouli is sometimes sold in an adulterated form that can cause skin irritation. Be sure to buy niaouli oil from a reputable dealer.

Aromatic medicinal plant members of the Myrtaceae family include eucalyptus (*Eucalyptus citriodora, E. dives, E. globulus,*

E. polybractea [cineole and krypton], *E. radiata*, *E. smithii*), clove (*Eugenia aromatica*, *E. caryophyllus*), tea tree (*Melaleuca alternifolia*), cajeput (*Melaleuca cajeputi*, *M. minor*), cajuput or cajeput (*Melaleuca quinquenervia* variety *nerolidol* and variety *cineolifera*), niaouli (*Melaleuca viridiflora*), green myrtle (*Myrtus communis*), and bay (*Pimenta racemosa*).

LAURACEAE

The Lauraceae family contains about 2,500 species and 45 genera. Many members of this family are commercially important as garden ornamentals, timber, and spices. Fragrant woods from sassafras and nectandra are used to make fine cabinets. The primary areas of distribution are in tropical and subtropical areas, primarily Brazil and Southeast Asia. The Lauraceae consist mainly of shrubs and trees with some parasitic herbaceous creepers. Common identifying characteristics of this family are simple, alternate leaves with leathery texture; strongly aromatic twigs, which contain the volatile oil; and insignificant flowers with numerous stamens.

Plants of the Lauraceae family are strongly antifungal, bactericidal, tonic, stimulant, and cell-regenerative, with antiviral properties. The Lauraceae have an affinity for the nervous system and are believed to be aphrodisiacs. Members of this family stimulate the cardiac, pulmonary, and circulatory systems. Therapeutic indications are hypotension, sexual debility, headaches, and depression. Members of this family with culinary uses are spices from cinnamon and bay leaf, and avocado from *Persea americana*.

Members of this family contain the constituent cinnamic aldehyde, which is a skin irritant found in the essential oils of cassia and cinnamon. Other members, which are toxic and not recommended for aromatherapy use, are camphor and sassafras, which contain the constituent safrole.

Aromatic medicinal plant members of the Lauraceae family are rosewood, bois de rose (*Aniba roseodora*), camphor (*Cinnamomum camphora*), cinnamon (*Cinnamomum zeylanicum, C. verum*), massoia aromatica (*Cryptocarya massoy*), bay laurel (*Laurus nobilis*), may chang (*Litsea cubeba*), ravensara (*Ravensara aromatica*), and North American sassafras (*Sassafras albidum*).

139

PINACEAE

The Pinaceae family contains 194 species and 9 genera. Many plants of this family are commercially important as garden ornamentals and timber. The Pinaceae's main areas of distribution are in the northern hemisphere and temperate climates.

The Pinaceae family consists mainly of shrubs and trees with opposite or whorled branches. This family is characterized by branches with evergreen needles that are aromatic and resinous, and male and female cones instead of flowering reproductive parts.

Plants of the Pinaceae family are highly antiseptic, tonic, revitalizing, and warming. The Pinaceae have an affinity for the respiratory, nervous, and endocrine systems. Therapeutic indications are arthritis, rheumatism, and stress. The Pinaceae are decongestants, stimulate deep breathing, and are very effective for respiratory disorders. Western larch tree (*Larix occidentalis*) has recently become part of alternative cancer therapy. *Larix* stimulates the activity of various immune cells, such as natural killer cells, which are very important in the prevention of new tumor growth in cancer patients.

Aromatic medicinal plant members of the Pinaceae family include Canada balsam, also called hemlock spruce (*Tsuga canadensis*); white fir (*Abies alba*); American silver fir, also called balm of Gilead (*Abies balsamea*); Siberian fir (*Abies siberica*); Atlantic cedar (*Cedrus atlantica*); black spruce (*Picea mariana*); larch (*Larix decidua*); turpentine pine (*Pinus pinaster*); and Scotch pine (*Pinus sylvestris*).

RUTACEAE

The Rutaceae family contains 1,650 species and 161 genera. This family is best known for citrus fruits, primarily oranges, lemons, and limes. Its main areas of distribution are in tropical climates and warm temperate climates, especially Africa and Australia.

The Rutaceae family mainly consists of shrubs and trees, with some herbaceous plants. This family is characterized by simple or compound leaves dotted with glands that contain the volatile oils. Flowers are usually five-petaled, often with twice the number of stamens as petals.

Citrus oils come from three different parts of the plant: the peel, the leaves, and the flowers. Most of the essential oils used in aromatherapy, such as orange, mandarin, lemon, bergamot, and grapefruit, are expressed from the peel. Petitgrain oils are extracted from the leaves of various citrus trees, most commonly the bitter orange. Neroli oil is distilled from the blossoms of the bitter orange tree.

The Rutaceae family is highly antiseptic, antispasmodic, tonic, and stimulating. The Rutaceae have an affinity for the digestive system and nervous system. Therapeutic indications are digestive disorders, nervousness, insomnia, and irritability. The flowers and leaves from *Citrus aurantium* relieve irritability and promote sleep. Bergamot aids digestion and relieves spasm in the stomach. The fruit of the Rutaceae regulate secretion of bodily fluids.

Citrus oils expressed from the peel contain flavonoids, pigments, and waxes that normally are not found in essential oils. These oils oxidize at a faster rate than other essential oils, which degrades the aldehydes into acids. Nitrogen gas is being used by some conscientious suppliers to displace the air in the storage bottles and thus lessen oxidation.

141

Members of the Rutaceae may be phototoxic when used on skin exposed to sun. Buchu and rue contain the constituent ketone, which is potentially toxic. Therefore, these oils are considered hazardous. Jaborandi is considered very toxic. These oils are not used in aromatherapy and should be avoided.

Aromatic medicinal plant members of the Rutaceae family include bitter orange, Seville orange (*Citrus aurantium* var. *amara, C. bigaradia, C. vulgaris*)—the source of bigarade oil, neroli bigarade oil, and petitgrain orange oil; bergamot (*C. bergamia, C. aurantium* subspecies *bergamia*); lime (*C. aurantifolia*); combava oil (*C. hystrix*); lemon (*C. limon*); grapefruit (*C. paradisi*); mandarin (*C. reticulata*); tangerine (*C. reticulata* var. *tangerine*); and sweet orange (*C. sinensis, C. aurantium* var. *sinensis*).

UMBELLIFERAE

The Umbelliferae family contains 3,100 species and 420 genera. This family is found worldwide, but most commonly in northern temperate climates. The Umbelliferae family consists mainly of annual, biennial, and perennial herbs with some shrubs; it is characterized by small flowers, often white or yellow in umbels; hollow stems between nodes; and often scented foliage.

This family contains many important plants used in aromatherapy. The Umbelliferae are also an important agricultural food source, with vegetables such as celery and carrots, and condiments and spices such as fennel, caraway, parsley, tarragon, cumin, and coriander.

Essential oils from this family are generally extracted from the seeds, which have been traditionally used as digestive aids in the form of aperitif liqueurs. The Umbelliferae family is carminative, antispasmodic, strengthening, and warming. The Umbelliferae have an affinity for the respiratory, digestive, and reproductive systems. Therapeutic indications are digestive upset, flatulence, spasms, and menstrual disorders such as cramps and painful periods.

Some Umbelliferae encountered in the field are very poisonous, such as water hemlock, so use caution when picking your own herbs. Some of the Umbelliferae contain potentially neurotoxic ketones; consult chapter 9 before use. In general, members of the Umbelliferae are considered phototoxic. Angelica root, tarragon, *Ammi visnaga*, and *Tagetes* should be used with caution when applied to skin exposed to sunlight.

Aromatic medicinal plant members of the Umbelliferae family include khella seed (*Ammi visnaga*), dill (*Anethum graveolens*), angelica (*Angelica archangelica*), celery (*Apium graveolens*), caraway (*Carum carvi*), chervil (*Anthriscus cerefolium*), gotu kola (*Centella asiatica*), cumin (*Cuminum cyminum*), carrot (*Daucus carota*), asafoetida (*Ferula foetida*), fennel (*Foeniculum vulgare*), lovage (*Levisticum officinale*), opopanax, parsley (*Petroselinum sativum*), and aniseed (*Pimpinella anisum*).

11

Aromatic
Materia Medica

ANGELICA
FAMILY: UMBELLIFERAE
Botanical name: *Angelica archangelica*

Angelica has a strong presence; it grows up to 6 feet tall. It is a
biennial or triennial plant. The leaves are bipinnate (divided into
secondary leaflets) or tripinnate (divided into tertiary leaflets)
with flowers in an umbel (a flower cluster with all the flowers
rising from one point, with the youngest bloom in the center).
Native to Europe and Siberia, it is now cultivated in Hungary,
Germany, and Belgium. This oil is held in high esteem by the
perfume industry for its peppery top note and earthy, herbaceous
aroma. A rather expensive oil: 340 pounds of plant material are
needed to produce 1 pound of essential oil.

Several varieties of angelica are used in Asian medicine. One of angelica's main uses in traditional Chinese medicine is to treat female disorders and infertility. This plant is considered second only to ginseng as a health-building tonic. In the Middle Ages, this oil was included in remedies said to extend life. Angelica rebuilds strength after any condition that depletes the body's life force. It is useful in convalescence after chronic illness, in cases of lowered immunity (it supports production of white blood cells), after childbirth, and to strengthen a weak heart.

Currently, angelica is listed in the *British Herbal Pharmacopoeia* as a specific for bronchitis associated with vascular insufficiency. A circulatory stimulant, it is useful for poor circulation in the lower extremities. Angelica has a long history of use in alleviating respiratory conditions such as colds, coughs, and sinus problems. For flu or viral or intestinal infections, 1 to 3 drops can be taken internally. Angelica is indicated for conditions that have become chronic.

In any type of digestive disorder, angelica should be a centerpiece in the treatment plan. Its calming effect on the nervous system relaxes spasms related to conditions such as diverticulosis and irritable bowel syndrome. This oil is beneficial for gastritis, dyspepsia, poor digestion, and gas.

Emotionally, angelica has a grounding effect for persons prone to anxiety. It has a calming, balancing, and sedative action on the nervous system and may have a supportive effect on the adrenal gland. It can be used as a nervine tonic in the form of baths or applied in a blend to the solar plexus.

Angelica root, when used topically on skin exposed to ultraviolet rays, may be phototoxic. Because of its coumarin content, internal use of this oil may interfere with anticoagulant drugs.

Medicinal Actions

Sedative, nervine, antispasmodic, carminative, anticoagulant, diuretic, expectorant, diaphoretic, depurative, digestive, stomachic, febrifuge, emmenagogue, tonic, stimulant

Conditions and Ailments

Colitis, flatulence, anxiety, nervous fatigue, insomnia, nasal polyps, infertility, cystitis, rheumatism, water retention

147

BERGAMOT
FAMILY: RUTACEAE
Botanical names: *Citrus bergamia, C. aurantium* subsp. *bergamia*

Bergamot's native home is Asia; it is now cultivated in Reggio di Calabria in southern Italy and in the Ivory Coast. Bergamot is a small tree that grows up to 16½ feet, with smooth, oval leaves. The fruit ripens from green to yellow and looks similar to small oranges. The essential oil is extracted by cold-pressing the rind of the fruit.

Bergamot has traditionally been used in Italy for intestinal worms and fever, especially intermittent types like that in malaria. Recent research in Italy has found this oil to be beneficial for respiratory infections, mouth problems, skin conditions, and urinary tract infections.

Bergamot has a fresh, uplifting aroma and has long been used to stabilize emotions. Studies have shown this oil balances the hypothalamus. Bergamot relieves tension and insomnia and is beneficial for anxiety and depression. It has the dual actions of both calming and tonifying the nervous system.

As a digestive aid, bergamot is carminative and spasmolytic, relieving symptoms of colic, gas, and indigestion. For these conditions, a blend of the oil can be massaged onto the abdomen in a clockwise direction, or 1 or 2 drops can be taken in honey. Bergamot stimulates appetite in persons with anorexia as well as balances the nervous system. For this condition, use as a massage blend, in a bath, or with an aroma lamp.

Bergamot is anti-infectious against a variety of microorganisms, including staphylococcus, gonococcus, meningococcus, and diphtheria bacilli. It is beneficial for genitourinary infections such as bladder infections (cystitis) and vaginitis; it can be used in a sitz bath for these conditions. (As an herbal complement to aromatherapy treatment for cystitis, a tea or extract of the herb uva-ursi can be taken along with unsweetened cranberry juice concentrate and plenty of fluids.)

For mouth problems and sore throats, bergamot can be used as a gargle: Add ⅛ teaspoon of salt and 3 drops of essential oil of bergamot to a half glass of warm water. This oil can be used for cold sores, rather than the more expensive melissa: Apply 1 drop of bergamot as needed.

Bergamot oil is considered phototoxic because it contains furocoumarins (bergaptene or 5-methoxypsoralen), substances that trap ultraviolet rays from the sun, then release them a short time later. Bergamot may actually have beneficial use in sun protection. Recent studies indicate that 5-methoxypsoralen (a component of furocoumarins) protects the skin from DNA damage and enhances tanning, especially in the fair-skinned.

Contraindications

External use may cause phototoxicity.

Medicinal Actions

Calming, sedative, stomachic, tonic, stimulant, digestive, carminative, febrifuge, antispasmodic, antiseptic, anti-infectious

149

Conditions and Ailments

Insomnia, nervous tension, depression, anxiety, colitis, colic, dyspepsia, flatulence, cystitis, vaginal discharge, fungus, colds, fever, flu, infections, mouth infections, poor appetite, anorexia, cramps, acne, oily skin, oily scalp, wounds, scabies, psoriasis, eczema, cold sores, insect bites, hemorrhoids

CARDAMOM
FAMILY: ZINGIBERACEAE
Botanical Name: *Elettaria cardamomum*

Cardamom is native to Asia and southern India; it is widely cultivated in India, Sri Lanka, Laos, Guatemala, and El Salvador. Cardamom is a perennial reedlike herb that grows up to 13 feet in height. It has long, silky, blade-shaped leaves with a rhizome similar to that of its relative, ginger; the flowers are small, and violet and yellow in color. The fruits are ovoid and contain three sections filled with the small reddish-brown seeds from which the essential oil is extracted. It has long been used in Asia as a culinary herb in curries, cakes, and garam masala.

Cardamom has been part of the Chinese and ayurvedic pharmacies for three thousand years. In China it was used for conditions of the lung because of its expectorant and decongestant properties. Cardamom is primarily a tonic to the digestive system. It is listed in the *British Herbal Pharmacopoeia* as a specific for flatulence and dyspepsia. This oil relieves spasm, making it beneficial for colitis, irritable bowel syndrome, indigestion, and cramps. Any digestive disorder in which nervous tension contributes to the condition will benefit from this oil. Cardamom relieves nausea and is useful for morning sickness in pregnancy: Inhale the aroma or have cardamom tea.

Cardamom is a tonic herb and is beneficial for weakness or emotional debility. It also strengthens weak digestion. It can be added to thyme and taken as a steam inhalant for congestion of the lungs.

This oil is a mild stimulant with a sensual quality. It is part of many aphrodisiac formulas in Asia. In general, essential oils that relieve muscle spasm and tone the digestive tract usually have similar effects on the smooth muscle of the reproductive system. It is a good essential oil to add to massage oil formulas for its warming properties and lovely, pleasant aroma.

Medicinal Actions

Tonic, stimulant, stomachic, antispasmodic, decongestant, expectorant, anti-infectious, antibacterial (variable), anthelmintic, carminative, digestive, nerve tonic, aphrodisiac

Conditions and Ailments

Poor digestion, dyspepsia, spastic colitis, colic, flatulence, bronchial catarrh, nervous debility

CHAMOMILE   151
FAMILY: ASTERACEAE
Botanical name: *Matricaria recutita; Anthemis nobilis*
Common name: *German chamomile; Roman chamomile*

German chamomile, a European native, is now cultivated in Egypt, Bulgaria, former Czechoslovakia, and Hungary. German chamomile is an annual herbaceous plant that grows 8 to 20 inches tall. It has furrowed stems with many branches; the leaves are bipinnate or tripinnate with yellow flowers. Roman chamomile grows to about 8 to 14 inches, with larger leaves. Many essential oils sold as chamomile are not true chamomile, but are actually Moroccan chamomile (*Tanacetum anum*) or *Ormenis mixta*.

Distilled German chamomile contains chamazulene, a byproduct of distillation. This chamazulene creates a deep blue color, which characterizes this oil. The medicinal actions of alpha-bisabolol, another important component in German chamomile, have been well researched and included antibacterial, antispasmodic, and vulnerary properties. Chamazulene and alpha-bisabolol are both strongly anti-inflammatory. Roman chamomile contains esters of acids, which are highly unusual in essential oil chemistry.

The wound-healing properties of chamomile have also been well researched. It affects a process called oxidative phosphorylation, which results in improved skin metabolism. The anti-inflammative effect of the essential oil applied topically promotes granulation (the formation of new capillaries on the surface of a wound during healing) and skin regeneration. German chamomile heals all types of skin conditions, such as allergic skin reactions, dermatitis, eczema, wounds, and abrasions. For burns, apply 1 or 2 drops and apply ice; the burned area will heal overnight.

Both Roman and German chamomile are known for their effects on the gastrointestinal system. Their combination of antispasmodic and anti-inflammative properties makes them effective remedies for digestive disorders such as dyspepsia, gas, spastic colon, diverticulosis, and gastritis. Because of its alpha-bisabolol content, German chamomile is an effective remedy for ulcers when taken as a tea, 2 to 3 cups a day. German chamomile used as gargle is beneficial for mouth problems such as stomatitis and gingivitis.

These oils are also nerve tonics, beneficial for nervous stomach and tension-related cramping. Roman chamomile soothes and calms the central nervous system, and a few drops massaged onto the solar plexus is considered helpful in relieving shock.

The chamomiles have been traditionally used for children's complaints. These oils are nontoxic and safe. For children's stomach aches, chamomile can be taken as a tea or gently massaged onto the abdomen.

Medicinal Actions

Anti-inflammatory, antispasmodic, carminative, stomachic, vulnerary, antibacterial

Conditions and Ailments

Stomatitis, cramps, flatulence, digestive disorders, colitis, ulcers, gallbladder problems, colic, skin disorders, sunburn, eczema, abscess, allergies, hives, gingivitis, stomatitis

153

CLARY SAGE
FAMILY: LAMIACEAE
Botanical name: *Salvia sclarea*

Clary sage, a native of Italy and Syria, prefers the dry, sunny climate of the Mediterranean region. It is now grown in Russia, Yugoslavia, Hungary, and France. Much of the clary sage available on the market is distilled in Crimea, Ukraine and is of good quality, although a higher grade of the oil is produced in Hungary and France.

Clary sage is a hardy plant that grows to 2 to 5 feet in height. Its opposite leaves are large, oblong with a cordate base, and downy. The flowers grow in terminal racemes (a flower cluster in which the individual flowers are attached by short stems, or pedicels, to an elongated unbranched main stalk, or axis, and in which the most mature blooms open from the top downward) and are lavender, blue, or pink.

Clary sage has a reputation for creating a sense of euphoria in the user. In times past, it was used in beer and wine making to heighten the effects of the alcohol. Clary sage is profoundly relaxing with a sensual quality. Its rich aroma is enjoyed by both men and women. It calms the parasympathetic nervous system and is a good remedy for nervous stress.

Clary sage contains 250 constituents, one of which, sclareol, has an estrogenlike structure, making clary sage beneficial for the female reproductive system. Sclareol has a hormone-balancing effect, which is useful for amenorrhea, cramps, and pain with menstruation. For relief of hot flashes in perimenopause, take a sponge bath with a few drops of clary sage in cool water. This oil also has a reputation for aiding sexual dysfunction, frigidity, and impotence. Massage with clary sage oil is very beneficial for these conditions, partly due to clary sage's hormonal influence and partly due to its ability to relieve anxiety and fear.

Clary sage is beneficial for nervous disorders, especially those accompanied by weakness and debility. Clary sage restores courage and confidence, making it useful in cases of postnatal depression, recovery from illness, and depression during illness. Its sedative qualities calm conditions of nervousness, fear, and anxiety.

This oil is a general tonic for the stomach and digestive system. Its antispasmodic properties relieve spasms and cramping in the digestive tract and diminish the tension that may be the cause. It is helpful for colic and gas pains in small children: Use a clary sage blend and gently massage the abdomen in a clockwise circular motion.

Clary sage is a general tonic and strengthens the entire body. It is ideal to use on a regular basis in baths or as perfume to revitalize and rejuvenate the body and mind.

Clary sage essential oil is generally considered nontoxic, but is not recommended for use in cases of active tumors or breast cancer.

Medicinal Actions

Antispasmodic, nervous system tonic, antidepressant, sedative, digestive aid, stomach tonic, carminative, uterine tonic, regenerative, general tonic

155

Conditions and Ailments

Amenorrhea, painful periods, sexual dysfunction, childbirth, PMS, dyspepsia, poor digestion, cramps, flatulence, epilepsy, depression, anxiety, and fear

EUCALYPTUS, GUM TREE
FAMILY: MYRTACEAE
Botanical name: *Eucalyptus globulus*

Eucalyptus is a native of Australia and is now cultivated in North America, Spain, France, Madagascar, Africa, India, Algeria, and Egypt. A tall, water-loving tree, it is often planted in areas in need of drainage. Eucalyptus is one of the tallest known trees, grow-ing to a height of 330 feet. The blue-green leaves are opposite with a leathery texture; oil glands are visible when the leaves are held to the light. The flower buds have lids that open when ready for pollination. They are fast-growing and invasive and now dominate parts of California's landscape. The hardwood is used for timber, and the essential oil is distilled from the leaves, twigs, and branches. About 50 pounds of plant material is needed to extract 1 pound of essential oil.

The realm of eucalyptus is respiration. It opens the lungs and encourages breathing by increasing oxygen in the cells, and it promotes the function of red blood cells. The strong antibac-terial and antiseptic properties of this plant make it ideal for any infectious condition. A small quantity of eucalyptus oil, when vaporized in a room, can kill 70 percent of the staphylococcus bacteria present. Eucalyptus expels mucus and is a remedy for sinusitis, coughs, colds, sore throat (use as a gargle), and all bronchial conditions. It has been used to treat tuberculosis and to prevent the spread of contagious disease. In its native land, eucalyptus leaves are dried and smoked as a remedy for asthma.

This oil is used to treat infectious conditions accompanied by fever. It has traditionally been used for malaria, cholera, and typhoid. The tea is used to treat bacterial dysentery. To reduce fever, compresses of the essential oil and cold water are applied to the legs. Eucalyptus is cooling in nature and should not be used if the patient feels chilled.

Eucalyptus is an excellent remedy for aching joints and rheumatism. It also reduces pain in sore muscles, sprains, and sports injuries. Topical application and baths are the treatments best suited for aches and pains.

Other varieties and types of eucalyptus used in aromatherapy include E. *polybractea*, E. *citriodora*, E. *radiata*, and E. *dives*.

Contraindications

Avoid use in infants.

Medicinal Actions

Expectorant, decongestant, prophylactic for respiratory conditions, antimicrobial, antibacterial, antiseptic, antiviral, antifungal, stimulant, vermifuge, insecticidal

157

Conditions and Ailments

Laryngitis, sore throat, otitis, bronchitis, asthma, flu, respiratory conditions, muscle pain, sprains, rheumatism, fever, headache, migraine, wounds, burns, debility

FRANKINCENSE (OLIBANUM)
FAMILY: BURSERACEAE
Botanical name: *Boswellia carteri*

Frankincense is native to the Red Sea region and grows wild throughout northeast Africa. It prefers an arid habitat. This tree or small shrub has pinnate leaves and light pink or white flowers. It yields a natural resin from which the essential oil is distilled. Workers collect the resin by making an incision in the bark, from which a white liquid exudes that forms tears of gum resin.

Frankincense has a long and revered use in religious ritual. In ancient times in Egypt, China, and India, it was burned as incense to enhance spiritual experience. The Catholic Church continues to use it today during the Mass. Frankincense is said to slow and deepen the breath, making it useful in meditation. For meditation, the essential oil can be burned in an aroma lamp.

The incense has health benefits as well. When burned, frankincense produces phenol (carbolic acid), a highly antiseptic substance used to disinfect the air. Burning frankincense in churches kept the buildings free of woodworm. The ancient Egyptians used it in cosmetics and as an ingredient in rejuvenating face masks.

158

In ayurvedic medicine, frankincense is called *salai guggul*. It has been used for centuries to treat many conditions, including arthritis. Modern science has isolated the active components of frankincense that have antiarthritic properties. These components, called boswellic acids, are effective because they inhibit the inflammatory process, improve blood supply, and prevent decreased cartilage synthesis.

In the modern botanical pharmacy, its anti-inflammative properties combined with anti-infectious properties are beneficial for many conditions. Frankincense is used as an expectorant in respiratory conditions, such as bronchitis and asthma. It is also useful for genitourinary tract infections, such as cystitis and leukorrhea.

Medicinal Actions

Expectorant, anticatarrhal, anti-inflammatory, cicatrizant, antidepressant, immunostimulant, possibly antitumoral, skin rejuvenator

Conditions and Ailments

Bronchitis, catarrh, asthma, nervous depression, immune deficiency, osteoarthritis, rheumatism, cystitis, leukorrhea, menorrhagia, blemishes, wrinkles, wounds, scars, ulcers, dry skin

GERANIUM
FAMILY: GERANIACEAE
Botanical names: *Pelargonium graveolens, P. odorantissimum*

In aromatherapy, the plant commonly called geranium is actually a pelargonium. Pelargoniums originated in South Africa and need to live in a climate where the temperature stays above freezing. They are now cultivated in Reunion (an island in the South Pacific), Madagascar, India, Guinea, and France. The plant grows to about 2 feet high, with serrated leaves and small pink flowers with five petals.

159

Geraniums are covered with glandular hairs that contain volatile oils. The essential oil is distilled from the leaves and stems just before or at flowering. The composition of the oil varies according to growing conditions.

Geraniums were used as traditional medicine in their native Africa by the peoples of Sothu and Xhosa, the Hottentots, and the Zulus for healing wounds, abscesses, sore throats, infections, fever, hemorrhoids, colds, and worms. Geranium is a relaxant, calming in cases of nervous tension and uplifting the spirits in depression.

Because of its ester content, geranium is a strong antifungal agent. It is effective against *Candida albicans* and does not disturb bacterial flora. Its antimicrobial activity may account for geranium's traditional use as a wound healer. The antibacterial properties of sixteen different commercial samples of geranium were tested on twenty-five types of bacteria. The growth of eight to nineteen types of bacteria was inhibited by the geranium oil. Geranium has traditionally been used against diarrhea and dysentery. Along with its anti-infectious properties, it is also anti-spasmodic to the smooth muscle tissue and astringent, affecting all aspects of this condition.

Often recommended for hormonal conditions such as menopause and female disorders, geranium may stimulate various glands. Used in the past for deficiency of the adrenal glands, it is now considered a stimulant for the function of the liver and pancreas. When applied to the breasts before and during menstruation, it can reduce the pain and swelling associated with PMS. Use 1 teaspoon essential oil of geranium to 2 ounces of carrier. Geranium also can be applied to stop excessive bleeding and hemorrhaging.

Geranium is also used as an insecticide against head lice. When sprayed on plants, it stops larvae from feeding. *Geranium macrorrhizum* is said to have antitumor properties and may be effective against certain cancers.

Aside from treating serious health conditions, geranium is a wonderful oil for skin care. Because of its antimicrobial properties, it is beneficial for hygienic maintenance when used in baths and applied to the skin as a blended oil. To disinfect the air and create a relaxing environment, diffuse geranium in an aromatherapy lamp.

Medicinal Actions

Analgesic, antimicrobial, antifungal, sedative, antispasmodic, relaxant, insecticidal, hemostatic, astringent, diuretic, tonic

Conditions and Ailments

Painful engorged breasts, uterine hemorrhage (decoction of leaves), diarrhea, gastric ulcer, nervous tension, depression, debility, wounds, sores, burns, herpes, shingles, dry eczema, tonsillitis, mouth conditions, stomatitis, fungal infections, *Candida albicans*, insect infestations (lice), edema of the legs

161

LAVENDER
FAMILY: LAMIACEAE
Botanical names: *Lavandula vera, L. officinalis, L. angustifolia*

Lavender's original home was southern France and Persia. Now it is cultivated in Yugoslavia, Italy, Spain, Morocco, and England. Wild lavender loves dry rocky soil and a high mountain altitude (between 2,600 and 5,000 feet) filled with sunshine. Its chemical constituents may vary according to the climate and altitude at which it is grown. It is harvested at the hottest time of day, and the essential oil is distilled from the fresh flowering tops.

L. vera/officinalis is a small shrub that grows 2 to 3 feet high with stiff stems. The leaves are evergreen and linear, with flowers in spikes that have a lovely violet-blue color. The flowers and leaves are strongly aromatic. *L. angustifolia* is a larger plant with many blossoms.

Lavenders are characterized by a high ester content preferred by the fragrance industry. It has become a usual practice for the adulterant synthetic ester linalyl acetate to be added to commercially sold lavender to meet the desired 40 percent of this constituent. The commercial lavender oils used to scent the many fragrant products on today's market contain only 3 percent real lavender. These "stretched" lavenders are used to scent potpourri, bath oil, and other products.

Lavender is highly regarded for its relaxing effect on the nervous system. This oil has an overall balancing effect on the state of mind and emotions. Lavender is a scent enjoyed by all, and its tension-relieving property is welcome after a stressful day in the modern world. It is especially effective added to a hot bath finished off with the application of a scented oil.

Lavender is one of aromatherapy's very useful essential oils, often called a "medicine chest in a bottle." It has many uses for treating everyday household and outdoor accidents. Keep it on hand at home and in a travel kit for insect bites, kitchen burns, cuts, bruises, wounds, sprains, dental pain, acne spots, sore throats, and aches and pains.

As a digestive aid, lavender stimulates the gastric secretions of the stomach and gallbladder. Taken before a meal, it reduces appetite by regulating the liver's blood-sugar output. As an immune system tonic, lavender stimulates white blood cell formation.

Lavender is antispasmodic to muscle tissue. It calms spasm in the solar plexus, an area of the body where many nerves converge. It is helpful in treating high blood pressure and relaxes cardiac spasms such as tachycardia. In general, lavender is used to relax muscle spasm anywhere in the body and to relieve pain. For headaches, apply a drop to the temples. For muscle spasm or cramps, blend with a carrier oil and massage the area. For arthritic aches and pains, apply compresses.

A hospital in Oxford, England, offers patients a choice between aromatherapy massage and night sedation—the majority choose aromatherapy. Patients report falling asleep just as easily, if not better, with lavender than with the drug temazepam (a benzodiazepine). In another Oxford hospital, lavender is used to enhance or replace pain medication. The staff has found that it works much faster than oral medication. Besides specific massage treatment with the oil, sprinkling a few drops of lavender on bedclothes or placing bowls of water with lavender oil around the ward helps patients sleep.

In British midwifery, lavender has been employed to relieve pain during labor and to aid in preparing the perineum (the area between the vagina and anus) for delivery. In a study of thirty-eight women giving birth, lavender baths were given during labor. Over half the women found the baths helpful in pain relief. Thirty-one women found the baths generally helpful, and thirty found them enjoyable. Another study was carried out with fifty-five first-time mothers, twenty-nine of whom performed perineal massage with lavender blended with a carrier oil for six weeks before birth. The massage group had a 48 percent rate of episiotomy and tearing, while the control group had a 77 percent rate.

Medicinal Actions

Antispasmodic, antiseptic, antimicrobial, insecticidal, sedative, nervine, analgesic, carminative, cholagogue, diuretic, vulnerary, regulating

Conditions and Ailments

Depression, insomnia, nervousness, mood swings, headache, pain, cramps, tachycardia, phlebitis, acne, skin care, abscess, eczema, burns, supportive to the spleen, rheumatism, nausea, motion sickness, fungal infections, yeast, athlete's foot, bronchitis, catarrh, flu, colds

MELISSA
FAMILY: LAMIACEAE
Botanical name: *Melissa officinalis*
Common names: Lemon balm, balm

164

This plant prefers well-drained soil in warmer climates. It originated in Asia and is now widely grown in the Mediterranean region, France, the Balkan states, and the United States. Melissa grows to about 2 feet, with small, hairy, serrated leaves and small, yellowish-white flowers. The essential oil is extracted from the herb, leaves, and flowers and is best harvested before or at the beginning of flowering.

Melissa oil is very expensive; 7½ to 3½ tons of plant is needed to yield 1 pound of essential oil. Because of its high cost, this oil is frequently adulterated with lemongrass and citronella oils. Its main chemical constituents are terpene aldehydes, neral, geraniol, citral, citronella, linalool, limonen, pinen, and various acids.

The word *melissa* is Greek for "honey bee." It is often planted near beehives, because it has a reputation for attracting bees and making delicious honey. Avicenna, the ancient Persian physician, called it "the elixir of life," and it was an ingredient of the famed Carmelite water created in 1379 by the Carmelite nuns. This cure-all water remained popular into the seventeenth century and was used to treat many conditions, including neuralgia, baldness, melancholy, and nervous headaches, and reputedly improved mental capacity and rejuvenated health.

Melissa concentrates in the hippocampus, which is located in the limbic system of the brain. This part of the brain affects our autonomic nervous system, emotions, endocrine function, and memory. Research has shown that the constituent aldehyde found in melissa has a sedative effect (interestingly, the aldehyde constituent alone is not as effective as the whole oil). Melissa's sedative action has a direct effect on the nervous system and limbic system, benefiting all conditions of nervous stress and making it an excellent remedy for anxiety and restlessness. For tension headaches, apply a drop to each temple. Melissa can also be used as a tea or an essential oil for emotional conditions, such as mild depression.

Melissa strengthens the heart. It is beneficial for stress-affected conditions of the heart, such as labile hypertension (blood pressure that rises under stress) and for nervous palpitations. This oil has been shown to cause some reduction of serum cholesterol with long-term use.

Melissa oil is a potent antiviral agent and is now used in various preparations to treat herpes and shingles. With only a few applications directly on the lesions, an outbreak can be ended (see pages 57–59 in chapter 5). Hydrosols of melissa have been found effective against influenza, smallpox, and mumps. German laboratories have found melissa to be effective against HIV (however, there is no evidence it can cure AIDS). Topically, melissa is anti-inflammative, thus useful for skin conditions related to allergy. Apply a compress for allergic eczema or dermatitis.

Melissa stimulates the liver and bile production. Bile is a natural laxative that benefits constipation and poor digestion from lack of digestive secretions. Because of its antispasmodic properties, this oil has long been used to relax the stomach and intestinal spasms. Melissa is carminative and aids in expelling gas and relieving gas pains.

Melissa has various actions on the thyroid gland, making it a promising treatment for hyperthyroidism. Research indicates that melissa extracts block the binding of stimulating immunoglobulins to the thyroid, which benefits autoimmune disorders such as Graves disease. Treatment with the essential oil rather than the extract may be equally effective.

Medicinal Actions

Antispasmodic, antiviral, anti-inflammatory, carminative, sedative, stomachic, antibacterial, hypothyroid activity (infused herb), choleretic

Conditions and Ailments

High blood pressure, asthma, eczema, menstrual disorders, irregular cycles, menopause, depression, insomnia, irritability, anxiety, headache, digestive disorders, dyspepsia, gastric spasm, flatulence, colic, heart disorders, palpitations, liver, gallbladder and spleen disorders, hyperthyroidism

NEROLI (ORANGE BLOSSOM)
FAMILY: RUTACEAE
Botanical names: *Citrus aurantium* var. *amara,*
Neroli bigarade, Citrus bigaradia

Neroli blossoms grow on the bitter orange tree; its native land is China. Now cultivated in Sicily, southern France, Tunisia, Morocco, and Egypt, this tree stands 18 to 33 feet high. The leaves are oval, pointed, dark-green, and glossy, with winged stems. The trunk is smooth and grayish. The flowers are small, white, and very fragrant. The blossoms are distilled or extracted by solvents to create neroli essential oil, sometimes called orange blossom oil. One ton of blossoms is needed to produce 1 quart of essential oil. Because of its low yield, neroli is one of the most expensive and most often adulterated essential oils.

167

Neroli is named after Anna Maria de La Tremoille, Princess of Nerola, who introduced this fragrance into Italian society, where it became a popular scent for personal items and the home.

Neroli is a sedative and tonic to the nervous system and beneficial for most disorders of emotional origin. It calms nervous spasm, making it a useful remedy for tachycardia (heart palpitations). This oil's sedative effect helps relieve insomnia and nervous excitability. It is useful for sudden shock or fear that may cause a strain on the heart: Inhale the essence with deep, slow breaths and massage a few drops over the solar plexus area.

Neroli has an affinity for the female reproductive system. It is a tonic to the uterus and relieves menstrual cramps. This oil can be used on a regular basis as a female tonic in baths and the blended oil can be topically massaged into the lower abdomen.

Neroli has been found to have antifungal properties and to be active against coli bacteria. Neroli is also anti-infectious for lung conditions, such as bronchitis and tuberculosis. Neroli is beneficial for intestinal parasite infections, such as giardia and ankylostomiasis. As a digestive aid, its antibacterial and antispasmodic properties make it an effective remedy for diarrhea. The digestive disorders nervous dyspepsia, colic, and irritable bowel syndrome often have a connection to nervous spasm. For these conditions, use neroli in the bath and massage the blended oil onto the abdomen in a clockwise direction to soothe tension. The hydrosol of neroli is very gentle, and it can be given to babies for colic: Use 1 teaspoon in a baby medicine dispenser.

168

Neroli's rich and lovely aroma make it an ideal scent for the home when used in an aroma lamp. The scent has great appeal and creates an air of tranquillity and relaxation. Worn as a perfume, it keeps the psyche from overreacting to stimuli and helps one to maintain a calm countenance.

Medicinal Actions

Anti-infectious, antibacterial (coli), antiparasitic, vascular tonic, digestive tonic, nervous tonic, antidepressant, antihypertensive, uterine tonic

Conditions and Ailments

Insufficiency of pancreas and liver, enterocolitis, diarrhea, parasites, bronchitis, pleurisy, nervous depression, fatigue, insomnia, sympathetic nervous system imbalance, tachycardia, spasm, cramps, hypertension, hemorrhoids, varicose veins

ROSEMARY

FAMILY: LAMIACEAE

Botanical name: *Rosmarinus officinalis*

Rosemary originated in the Mediterranean region. Now it is grown in France, Italy, Spain, Yugoslavia, Tunisia, and California. This plant is shrublike and bushy, with stiff, leathery, evergreen, needlelike leaves; the flowers are small and light blue; and the whole plant is strongly aromatic. The oil is distilled from the fresh flowering tops and upper part of the herb. Rosemary is one of the most commonly adulterated essential oils; one can only be sure of getting the real thing if the seller knows the source of distillation.

Rosemary stimulates the central nervous system and circulatory system. It is beneficial for low blood pressure, or when a person has cold extremities, is sluggish, and is in a deficient condition (a weakened, fragile state with lowered metabolic function). The *British Herbal Pharmacopoeia* lists rosemary as a specific for depressive states with general debility and cardiovascular weakness. It can be added to formulas for which a circulatory tonic is indicated or to add warming and stimulating qualities to the blend.

When depression is accompanied by stagnation and immobility, rosemary can help uplift the spirits. For sluggishness, try a brisk rosemary rubdown in the shower: Put 2 to 3 drops on a washcloth with shower gel and massage over the body from the feet up. This oil is considered a cerebral stimulant; it strengthens mental awareness. It has a long reputation of helping poor memory, not only by stimulating the brain but by increasing blood flow. It is useful for mental fatigue when working long hours or studying: Diffuse the oil or periodically inhale the essence.

169

Rosemary has traditionally been used for rheumatic pains, stiff joints, and sore muscles. Use as a topical application by blending with essential oils of black pepper and lavender and a carrier oil, or apply a compress with rosemary oil to the area.

Rosemary is an all-purpose remedy for respiratory conditions. It contains the chemical constituent cineol, which gives rosemary its expectorant and mucolytic properties. This oil is strongly bactericidal against *Staphylococcus*, *Streptococcus*, *E. coli*, *Proteus*, and *Klebsiella*. It is also fungicidal against *Candida albicans*. Catarrh, sinusitis, otitis, bronchitis, and lung infections benefit from its antiseptic and anti-infectious properties. Rosemary is best used to treat respiratory conditions with steam inhalation, diffusion, and topical application with a carrier oil.

170

Rosemary is beneficial as a carminative, relieving gas and painful digestion. Its anti-infectious properties are effective against bacterial diarrhea.

Rosemary verbenone is a chemotype of rosemary. It has mucolytic and digestive properties similar to those of the rosemary cineol type. Rosemary verbenone contains ketones, which are cell-regenerative. It is especially good for skin care and healing scar tissue.

Contraindications

Do not use excessive dosage. Avoid in cases of epilepsy. Rosemary chemotype verbenone should not be used by children or pregnant women.

Medicinal Actions

Expectorant, mucolytic, antibacterial, antifungal, antiseptic, antitussive, stimulant, cholagogue, nervous system tonic, cerebral stimulant, stimulates menstruation, cicatrizant, diaphoretic, diuretic, digestive, stomachic, carminative, hair care

Conditions and Ailments

Bronchitis, whooping cough, otitis, sinusitis, asthma, flu, colds, coughs, colitis, dyspepsia, liver conditions, jaundice, gallbladder inflammation, gout, cystitis, high cholesterol, rheumatism, sore muscles, low blood pressure, poor circulation, mental fatigue, migraine, poor memory, alopecia (stimulates hair growth)

171

TEA TREE
FAMILY: MYRTACEAE
Botanical name: *Melaleuca alternifolia*

Melaleuca alternifolia is a tree native to New South Wales, Australia. It is harvested as wild trees and as cultivars (a type of plant originating and persistent under cultivation) in recent plantations. It has feathery, narrow, bright-green leaves, with heads of yellowish or purple flowers. It prefers swampy terrain and is hardy and extremely disease resistant. The essential oil is distilled from the leaves. This tree thrives on harvesting; pruning stimulates rapid new growth.

The Bundjalung Aborigines in northeastern New South Wales have used tea tree as a healing herb for hundreds of years. They treat skin infections, cuts, and wounds by making a poultice of the leaves, placing it on the wound, then covering it with a mud pack.

The standard for chemical composition of tea tree oil is more than 30 percent terpinen-4-ol and less than 15 percent cineole. Tea tree oil appears to be effective against infectious microbes like *Candida albicans* because of this composition. This low cineole content also appears to render this oil safe and nontoxic. A wonderful aspect of tea tree oil is that it fights infection without harming healthy tissue. In other oils, such as eucalyptus, cineole is responsible for toxic and irritant effects.

172

Tea tree oil's major contribution to aromatherapy is its broad spectrum of antimicrobial activity. Its anti-infectious ability is beneficial in cases of bacterial, viral, protozoal, and fungal infection. Tea tree oil is five times stronger than typical household disinfectants and twelve times stronger than carbolic acid. Tea tree oil has been found effective against *Staphylococcus aureus*, *Escherichia coli*, *Trichophytia*, *Streptococcus*, *Candida albicans*, *Pseudomonas aeruginosa*, *Proteus vulgaris*, *Pneumococcus*, *Gonococcus*, *Meningococcus*, *Diphtheria bacterium*, and *Aspergillus niger*. This oil is also effective against antibiotic-resistant strains of *Staphylococcus aureus*.

Often called a "first-aid kit in a bottle," it is the ideal oil to take along on camping trips, hiking, or any other travel adventures. Tea tree oil has the added benefit of being the best mosquito repellent I have ever used. To repel insects, apply a few drops neat to the back of the neck, knees, and on the arms. Tea tree can be used on abrasions, cuts, and wounds, even if the wound is unclean. In fact, blood and pus appear to increase the effectiveness of tea tree oil by 10 percent. The oil dissolves pus and is an effective disinfectant wash when mixed with water in a 10 percent dilution. Tea tree oil has antitoxic properties and appears to neutralize the effect of some poisonous spider bites, such as that of Australia's funnel spider, whose venom toxicity is similar to that of the black widow spider.

Tea tree oil is an all-purpose remedy for respiratory infections, not only acting as an anti-infective agent but also increasing the body's ability to fight infection by strongly stimulating immune function. For respiratory conditions, use as a gargle, as an inhalant, or topically in a carrier oil.

Fungal infections such as ringworm and athlete's foot are rapidly healed with topical application of tea tree. Dandruff is commonly caused by a fungus: Add tea tree oil to shampoo or apply topically mixed with a carrier, and leave on overnight. For nailbed fungus, which is often caused by *Candida*, apply 1 or 2 drops neat under the nail two or more times a day.

Tea tree oil is beneficial for genital infections such as herpes, vaginitis, trichomonas, and *Candida albicans*. For vaginal yeast, there are several methods of application: tea tree suppositories (available at health-food stores) or douches. Dilute tea tree with water or make an oil blend (be sure to use a plastic syringe to insert the oil into the vagina).

Tea tree has been found effective against chronic cystitis. In a double-blind trial, twenty-six female patients were given tea tree oil internally. Seven were cured (for a chronic condition, this is considered significant). Karen Cutter, a Sydney, Australia, naturopath, successfully treated patients suffering from systemic

Candida associated with AIDS. The patients took doses of up to 60 drops per day with no apparent ill effects.

Medicinal Actions

Broad-spectrum antimicrobial, antiseptic, antibacterial, antifungal, antiparasitic/protozoal, anti-inflammatory, immunostimulant, expectorant, antitoxic, ovarian decongestant, venous decongestant

Conditions and Ailments

174

Insect bites, spider bites, burns, wounds, cuts, abrasions, impetigo, acne, *Candida* infections, vaginal infections, yeast, trichomonas, genital herpes, urinary tract infections, respiratory infections, bronchitis, throat infection, sinus infections, lice, dandruff, ringworm, athlete's foot, mouth sores, mucous membrane infections, cold sores, gum infections, gingivitis, pyorrhea, enterocolitis, boils, abscesses, warts, varicose ulcers, diaper rash

THYME
FAMILY: LAMIACEAE
Botanical name: *Thymus vulgaris*

Thyme is a native of the Mediterranean region and prefers a sunny climate with well-drained soil. It is a small shrub that grows to a foot high with woody, opposite multiple branches. The young shoots are purplish-red and pubescent; the leaves are opposite, oval, and smooth, with oil glands. The flowers are small, pale purple or white, polygamous, arranged in a cyme (a flower cluster in which the central flower is the oldest) in the uppermost axils of the leaves. The essential oil is distilled from the flowering tops.

Thyme has been in use as a medicinal plant since ancient times. In Greek, the word *thyme* means "courage," and indeed the strength of this botanical in herbal medicine is well reputed. In the *British Herbal Pharmacopoeia*, thyme is indicated for dyspepsia, chronic gastritis, bronchitis, pertussis (whooping cough), asthma, children's diarrhea, laryngitis, tonsillitis, and bedwetting in children.

Thyme has primarily been used for digestive and respiratory ailments. It relaxes the smooth muscle of the intestine, which helps expel gas and relieve spasms in colic. In respiratory conditions thyme is antiseptic and a bronchodilator and expectorates mucus from the lungs. Thyme helps reduce fever by inducing sweat. The herb has been used to fight tooth infection and toothache.

Some researchers speculate that thyme's antibacterial effect may help sufferers of ankylosing spondylitis, a progressive disease of the hip joints, lower back, and spine. People with spondylitis have high levels of *Klebsiella* bacteria. Thyme is effective against *Klebsiella*.

The chemical constituents of thyme essential oil vary; these varieties are called chemotypes. *Thymus vulgaris* chemotype (ct.) thymol is rich in phenols (thymol and carvacrol), making this a strongly antibacterial oil suitable for acute infections. It can be an irritant and should not be used topically.

T. vulgaris ct. thuyanol contains alcohols and is effective against many infectious conditions such as flu, bronchitis, vaginitis, and cervicitis. It stimulates the regeneration of liver cells, stimulates immune response, is antiviral, and is effective against chlamydia. With its broad range of effects against infectious conditions, this is a good oil to keep in the medicine chest for general family health care. It is beneficial for stomatitis, otitis, sinusitis, bronchitis, nervous disorders, cystitis, vaginitis, infections of the female reproductive system, and prostatitis. Thyme thujanol oil is mild and has no contraindications.

Contraindications

Avoid use if you have high blood pressure. Some thymes are high in potentially toxic phenols; see chapter 9 before use. Topical use can cause irritation.

Medicinal Actions

Expectorant, antiseptic, bactericidal, anthelmintic, diaphoretic, antispasmodic, stomachic, carminative, stimulant, antitussive, antitoxic, emmenagogue, tonic, nerve tonic, parasitic, vermifuge

Conditions and Ailments

Asthma, bronchitis, coughs, congestion, laryngitis, sore throat, tonsillitis, sinusitis, rheumatism, arthritis, poor circulation, edema, aches and pains, diarrhea, dyspepsia, flatulence, cystitis, urethritis, infections, flu, cough, colds, chills, insomnia, nervous debility, abscess, gum infections

GLOSSARY

Alopecia: Balding.

Amenorrhea: Absence of menstruation after menarche and before menopause.

Analgesic: Substance that relieves pain.

Anthelmintic: Agent that destroys or expels worms.

Anticoagulant: Agent that delays or prevents blood clotting.

Anti-inflammative: Substance that reduces inflammation such as swelling, heat, and redness.

Antiphlogistic: Anti-inflammative.

Antipyretic: Agent that reduces fever.

Antiseptic: Substance that inhibits the growth of bacteria.

Antispasmodic: Relieves smooth muscle spasm (spasmolytic).

Antitussive: Soothes coughs.

Carminative: Expels gas and calms digestive spasms.

Catarrh: Inflammation of the mucous membranes accompanied by excessive discharge of mucus.

Cholagogue: Increases bile flow.

Cicatrizant: Encourages the formation of scar tissue, helps heal wounds.

Colitis: Inflammation of the colon.

Cyme: An inflorescence with the central flower being the oldest.

Cystitis: Urinary tract infection.

Depurative: Cleansing properties; purifies by the removal of toxic waste.

Diaphoretic: Induces perspiration.

Digestive: Aids digestion.

Diuretic: Relieves excess fluids through urination.

Dysmenorrhea: Painful menstruation.

Dyspepsia: Poor digestion, usually accompanied by heartburn or regurgitation of stomach acids.

Edema: Fluid retention.

Emmenagogue: An agent that brings on menstruation.

Endocrine: Pertaining to the hormonal system.

Enfleurage: A method of extracting essential oils from highly fragrant flowers that are pressed numerous times into layers of fat.

Enuresis: Bedwetting.

Expectorant: Agent that facilitates expulsion of mucus from the lungs and respiratory tract.

Febrifuge: Reduces fever.

Fixed oils: Lipids that contain long-chain fatty acids; vegetable oils.

Flatulence: Excessive gas from the intestines or stomach.

Hemostatic: Stops bleeding.

Homeostasis: State of balance.

Homologue: Substance with similar properties; a substitute.

Hypotensor: Lowers blood pressure.

Inflorescence: A grouping of flowers; a flowerhead.

179

Leukorrhea: Vaginal discharge associated with infection.

Menorrhagia: Excessive bleeding at menstruation, in either amount or duration.

Mucolytic: Dissolves and loosens mucus.

Neat: Undiluted.

Nervine: Tonic and soothing to the nervous system.

Olfaction: The process of perceiving smell.

Otitis: Middle ear infection.

Phagocytes: Immune cells that absorb foreign material and debris.

Phenylpropane derivative: Chemical grouping of components contained in essential oils.

Progesterone: A female hormone secreted after ovulation by the corpus luteum.

Raceme: An inflorescence on which individual flowers are attached by short stems (pedicels) to an elongated unbranched main stalk (axis). In most cases, the flowers open from the base upward.

Sitz bath: A tub to bathe in, in which only the hips are submerged in water.

Spasmolytic: Relieves spasms or convulsions.

Stomachic: Tonic of the stomach.

Stomatitis: Inflammatory disease of the mouth.

Sudorific: Agent that induces perspiration.

Tachycardia: Abnormally fast heartbeat.

Terminal raceme: A raceme in which the most mature flowers open from the top downward.

Terpene: A primary chemical contained in essential oils.

Tonic: An agent that tones and revitalizes the body or systems of the body.

Vermifuge: Agent that expels intestinal worms.

Volatile oil: Aromatic, oxygenated derivative of terpenes distilled from plants.

Vulnerary: An agent applied externally that assists in wound healing.

RESOURCES

ASSOCIATIONS

NAHA
National Association of Holistic
  Aromatherapy
836 Hanley Industrial Court
St. Louis, MO
1-888-ASK-NAHA

ESSENTIAL OILS

**Pacific Institute of
  Aromatherapy**
P.O. Box 6842
San Rafael, CA 94903
(415) 459-3998

**Snow Lotus Aromatherapy,
  Inc.**
875 Alpine Ave., Suite 5
Boulder, CO 80304
1-800-682-8827 or
(303) 443-9289

Aroma Vera
5901 Rodeo Rd.
Los Angeles, CA 90016
1-800-699-9154 or
(310) 280-0407

Aroma Clinic
e-mail: FloraMare@aol.com

Aromatherapy and herbal
formulas

AROMATHERAPY COURSES

The Laboratory of Flowers
4218 N. Glencoe
Marina Del Rey, CA 90292
1-800-677-2368 or
(310) 827-7737
Michael Scholes, Director

Seminars, retail essential oils, and
aromatherapy products

**Pacific Institute of
  Aromatherapy
  The Aromatherapy
  Correspondence Course**
P.O. Box 6842
San Rafael, CA 94903
(415) 459-3998

**Artemis Institute of Natural
Therapies**
875 Alpine Ave., Suite 5
Boulder, CO 80304
(303) 443-9289

182

COURSES IN HERBAL MEDICINE

**Pacific School of Herbal
  Medicine**
P.O. Box 3151
Oakland, CA 94609
(510) 845-4028

**Southwest School of
  Botanical Medicine**
P.O. Box 4565
Bisbee, AZ 85603
(520) 432-5855
Michael Moore, Director

HERBS

Tierona's Herbals
4840 Pan American East FWY NE
Albuquerque, NM 87109-2220
1-800-553-7720 or
(505) 553-4165

SUPPLIES

Netti Pots
The Himalayan Institute
1-800-822-4547

RECOMMENDED READING

BOOKS

Avila, Elena. *Woman Who Glows in the Dark*. New York: Penguin Putnam, 1998.

Bove, Mary. *An Encyclopedia of Natural Healing for Children and Infants.* Los Angeles: Keats Publishing, 1996.

———. *Herbs for Women's Health*. Los Angeles: Keats Publishing, 1997.

Fischer-Rizzi, Susanne. *Complete Aromatherapy Handbook*. New York: Sterling Publishing, 1990.

Lavabre, Marcel. *Aromatherapy Workbook*. Rochester, Vt.: Healing Arts Press, 1990.

Lawless, Julia. *The Encyclopedia of Essential Oils*. Longmead, Dorset, England: Element Books, 1995.

Moore, Martha. *Beyond Cortisone*. Los Angeles: Keats Publishing, 1998.

Moore, Michael. *Medicinal Plants of the Pacific West*. Santa Fe, N. Mex.: Red Crane Books, 1993.

Pert, Candace. *Molecules of Emotion*. New York: Scribner Publishing, 1997.

Schnaubelt, Kurt. *Advanced Aromatherapy*. Rochester, Vt.: Healing Arts Press, 1998.

JOURNALS

International Journal of Aromatherapy (IJA)
Harcourt Brace
P.O. Box 156
Avenel, NJ 07001
(877) 479-5032

Robyn's Recommended Reading
Sweetgrass Herbs
1627 Main St., Suite 116
Bozeman, MT 59715
(406) 585-8006

Reviews of books about herbs and botanical medicine.

REFERENCES

Ackerman, Diane. *A Natural History of the Senses*. New York: Vintage Books, 1990.

Actander, Stephen. *Perfume and Flavors of Natural Origin*. Las Vegas: Stephen Actander Publishing, 1982.

Aromatherapy World (summer 1992).

Austra-Asian College. Module 10. Auckland: Austra-Asian College.

Avery, Alexandra. *Aromatherapy and You*. Portland, Maine: Blue Heron Hill Press, 1994.

Baumgardt, John Phillip. *How to Identify Flowering Plants*. Portland, Maine: Timber Press, 1982.

Bove, Mary. *Herbs for Women's Health*. Los Angeles: Keats Publishing, 1997.

Brown, Donald. *Herbal Prescriptions for Better Health*. Rocklin, Calif.: Prima Publishing, 1996.

Burton Group. *Alternative Medicine*. Tiburon, Calif.: Future Medicine Publishing, 1997.

Davis, Patricia. *Aromatherapy A–Z*. Saffron Walden, England: C.W. Daniel Co., Ltd., 1988.

Diamond, W. John, and W. Lee Cowden. *Cancer.* Tiburon, Calif.: Future Medicine Publishing, 1997.

Drury, Susan. *Tea Tree Oil.* Saffron Walden, England: C. W. Daniel Co., Ltd., 1991.

Ericksen, Marlene. "Diverticulosis." *International Journal of Aromatherapy* 5, no. 2 (summer 1993): 31–32.

Fischer-Rizzi, Susanne. *Complete Aromatherapy Handbook.* New York: Sterling Publishing, 1990.

Franchome, Pierre. *L'Aromatherapie Exactement.* Edited by Roger Jollois. Limoges, France: Roger Jollois, 1990.

Gattefosse, Rene-Maurice. *Gattefosse's Aromatherapy.* Saffron Walden, England: C. W. Daniel Co., Ltd., 1993.

Graces, Ulla-Majia. *Aromatherapy for Practitioners.* Saffron Walden, England: C. W. Daniel Co., Ltd., 1996.

Graham, Judy. *Evening Primrose Oil.* Rochester, Vt.: Healing Arts Press, 1984.

Hampton, Aubrey. *Natural Organic Hair and Skin Care.* Tampa, Fla.: Organica Press, 1987.

Herbalgram 46 (spring 1999).

Hoffman, David. *The New Holistic Herbal.* Longmead, Dorset, England: Element Books, 1990.

Holmes, Peter. "Neroli." *The International Journal of Aromatherapy* 7, no. 2 (1995): 16.

International Journal of Aromatherapy 1, no. 1, 2, and 4, (winter/spring double issue 1998–1999): 11.

ISPA. "Melissa." *Aromatherapy World* (autumn 1993).

J. Paul Getty Museum. *Ancient Herbs.* Malibu, Calif.: The J. Paul Getty Museum. 1982.

Lake, Max. *Scents and Sensuality.* London: John Murray, 1989.

Lavabre, Marcel. *Aromatherapy Workbook.* Rochester, Vt.: Healing Arts Press, 1990.

Lawless, Julia. *The Encyclopedia of Essential Oils.* Longmead, Dorset, England: Element Books, 1995.

———. *Aromatherapy and the Mind.* Boston: Thorson's Publishing, 1994.

Lis-Balchin, Maria. "Geranium Oil." *The International Journal of Aromatherapy* 7, no. 3 (1996).

Litovitz, Toby L. "1998 Annual Report of the American Association of Poison Control Centers Toxic Exposure Surveillance System." *American Journal of Emergency Medicine* 17, no. 5 (1999): 435–87.

Lowdog, Tierona. *Foundations in Herbal Medicine.* Albuquerque, N.Mex.: Tierona Lowdog, 1998.

Mabberly, D. J. *The Plant Book.* Cambridge, Mass.: Cambridge University Press, 1996.

Mabey, Richard. *The New Age Herbalist.* New York: Collier Books, 1988.

Majno, Guido. *The Healing Hand.* London: Harvard University Press, 1991.

Mannicche, Lise. *An Ancient Egyptian Herbal.* Austin: University of Texas Press, 1989.

Milne, Robert, and Blake Moore. *Definitive Guide to Headaches.* Tiburon, Calif.: Future Medicine Publishing, 1997.

The Monell Connection (spring 1996). Newsletter.

Moore, Michael. *Herbal Repertory in Clinical Practice.* Albuquerque, N.Mex.: Southwest School of Botanical Medicine, 1991.

Morris, Edwin. *Fragrance.* Greenwich, N.Y.: E.T. Morris and Co., 1984.

Murray, Michael, and Joseph Pizzorno. *Encyclopedia of Natural Medicine.* Rocklin, Calif.: Prima Health, 1998.

Nissim, Rina. *Natural Healing in Gynecology.* New York: Pandora, 1986.

Olsen, Cynthia. "Tea Tree Oil." *Beyond Scents* 1, no. 3: 7–8,

Pacific Institute of Aromatherapy. Proceedings of the PIA Third Aromatherapy Conference, 1998, 53.

———.Conference notes, 1995.

Price, Len. "Frankincense." *Aromatherapy World* (winter 1991): 12.

Reader's Digest. *Magic and Medicine of Plants.* Pleasantville, N.Y.: The Reader's Digest Association, 1990.

Reeves, Carole. *Egyptian Medicine.* Buckinghamshire, England: Shire Egyptology, 1992.

Ryman, Daniele. *Aromatherapy.* New York: Bantam Books, 1993.

Schnaubelt, Kurt. *Advanced Aromatherapy.* Rochester, Vt.: Healing Arts Press, 1998.

———.*The Aromatherapy Course.* San Rafael, Calif.: Dr. Kurt Schnaubelt, 1985.

Sellar, Wanda. *The Directory of Essential Oils.* Saffron Walden, England: C. W. Daniel, Co., Ltd. 1992.

Sheppard-Hanger, Sylla. *The Aromatherapy Practitioner Manual.* Tampa, Fla: The Atlantic Institute of Aromatherapy, 1995.

Shirley, Price. *Aromatherapy for Health Professionals.* London: Churchill Livingstone, 1995.

Svoboda, Robert, and Arnie Lade. *Tao and Dharma.* Twin Lakes, Wis.: Lotus Press, 1995.

187

Tisserand, Robert. *Aromatherapy for Everyone*. London: Penguin Books, 1988.

————. *The Essential Oil Safety Data Manual*. Brighton, Sussex, England: The Association of Tisserand Aromatherapists, 1985.

————. *The Art of Aromatherapy*. New York: Destiny Books, 1983.

————. "Tea Tree Oil." *The International Journal of Aromatherapy* 1, no. 2 (1988): 7–8.

Tiwari, Maya. *Ayurveda: Secrets of Healing*. Twin Lakes, Wis.: Lotus Press, 1995.

Valnet, Jean. *The Practice of Aromatherapy*. New York: Destiny Books, 1980.

Wallis Budge, E. A. *Herb Doctors and Physicians in the Ancient World*. Chicago: Ares Publishing, 1927.

Weiss, Rudolph. *Herbal Medicine*. Beaconsfield, London: Beaconsfield Publishing, Ltd., 1988.

Williams, L., V. Homes, and S. Asre. "Oils of *Malaleuca Alternifolia*." *International Journal of Aromatherapy* 2, no. 4 (1990): 12–13.

Worwood, Valerie. *The Complete Book of Essential Oils & Aromatherapy*. Novato, Calif.: New World Library, 1991.

Yarnell, Eric. "Topical Essential Oils Successfully Treat Alopecia." *Health Notes* 6, no. 2 (summer 1999): 77.

Zomlefer, Wendy. *Flowering Plant Families*. Chapel Hill: University of North Carolina Press, 1994.

INDEX

194

essential fatty acids, 82
essential oils
　absorption into circulatory
　　system, 15
　application methods, 4-5
　benefits of, 3
　blending with carriers, 29-36
　buying, 22-27
　chemistry of, 21-22
　complete, necessity for, 24
　contraindications for, 132-133
　diffusion into air, 4
　effective at many levels, 5-6
　emotions and mind and, 13
　extraction of, 2-3, 18-21
　purposes in nature and in
　　aromatherapy, 17-18
　quality of, 3, 19, 22-26
　safety and toxicity of, 125-134
　shelf life, 44
　sources of, 2, 17
　standard dilution, oil to carrier,
　　30, 39, 43
　steam distillation of, 9
　worn as fragrance, 4
esters, 18, 21, 26
eucalyptus, 4, 5-6, 22, 53, 56, 57,
　　73, 106, 107, 108, 127,
　　137, 138
　about, 155-157
evening primrose, 81, 94
everlasting, 61
exercise, Warm-Up Oil for, 63
Expectorant/Mucolytic
　　Formula, 77
expectorant oils, 22, 72-73
extraction methods, 18-21
Eyes, Puffy, Treatment for, 115

F

facial and body oil beauty
　　blends, 116-118
Facial Clearing Steam for Acne,
　　87
Facial Steam, 111
facial steam, 37
facial treatments, natural, 111-118
families, aromatic, 135-143
farming practices, 25-26
fennel, 7, 48, 57, 90, 91, 93, 127,
　　143
fenugreek, 83
fertile periods, 14
fever, 107
flu, 57, 107
　humidifiers for, 37
　prevention of, 74
folic acid, 79
foot, blood vessels in, 41
foot baths, 41-42
foot massage, 67
　Antidepressant Foot Massage
　　Blend, 69
fragrances of essential oils, 17,
　　39-40
France, 2, 22-23, 25
　regulation of essential oils in,
　　23-24
Franchome, Pierre, 2, 9-10
frankincense, 7, 8, 9
　about, 157-159
fungicidal oils, 73-74

195

203